CAPE COD'S
COOKING SECRETS

Starr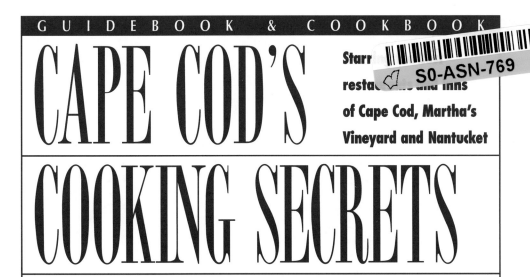 restaurants and inns of Cape Cod, Martha's Vineyard and Nantucket

By Kathleen DeVanna Fish

Bon Vivant Press
Monterey, California

Library of Congress Cataloguing-in-Publication Data

CAPE COD'S COOKING SECRETS
Starring the best restaurants and inns of
Cape Cod, Martha's Vineyard and Nantucket

First printing 1993

Fish, Kathleen DeVanna
93-070482
ISBN 0-9620472-9-5
$14.95 softcover
Includes indexes
Autobiography page 254

Editorial direction by Fred Hernandez
Cover photography by Robert N. Fish
Cover design by Morris Design
Inn and map drawings by Elna Mira Bjorge—Ultimate Productions
Illustrations by Robin Brickman, pages 6, 7
Historical photos from the Dukes County Historical Society
and the Joseph A. Nickerson Collection
Type by Electra Typography

Published by Bon Vivant Press,
a division of The Marketing Arm
P.O. Box 1994
Monterey, CA 93942

Printed in the United States of America
by Publishers Press

Contents

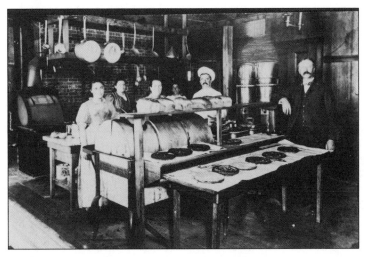

Harbor View Hotel kitchen, circa 1899. At right is Frank A. Douglas, owner and manager.

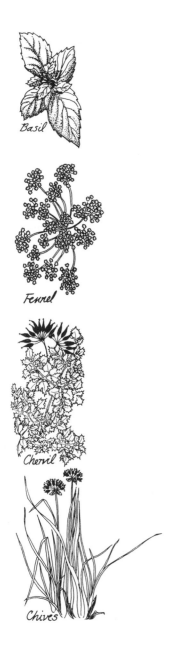

Basil

Fennel

Chervil

Chives

Everybody agrees: Cape Cod, Martha's Vineyard and Nantucket is an area full of beauty, charm, a colorful history—and exquisite dining. The purpose of this guidebook/cookbook is to offer you inside information on the best restaurants and inns, as well as the secret recipes of the top chefs. And to tempt you to savor the areas' rich flavors even after you return home.

"Cape Cod's Cooking Secrets" features 54 great chefs and 145 kitchen-tested recipes that exemplify the best cooking in New England. The menus and recipes assembled in this collection have been contributed by some of New England's most talented chefs. Nobody paid to be included in this book—the restaurants and inns were hand-selected and invited to participate.

The closely guarded recipes draw on the secrets of the chefs. Some come from their menus, some come from the chefs' private repertoires. We were after the finest food in the entire region. And just in case you can't get the same ingredients at home, we offer a mail-order food guide.

The very selective list of restaurants includes some that are elegant, some that are comfortably casual and some that the locals would prefer to keep to themselves. Also included are recommendations for unforgettable places to stay—inns whose heritage and purpose are unique. Each was chosen because it is so enchanting, so perfect in ambiance and service that you will luxuriate in the surroundings.

Selections include treasured recipes from the inns. The restaurants go one step further: they provide full menus and their secret recipes. The format is easy to follow with preparation times ranging from 15 minutes to three hours.

But we offer more than that. "Cape Cod's Cooking Secrets" provides a historical perspective that overlaps what every visitor should know to fully enjoy a visit. Every area is introduced with a map, historical highlights, local lore and tips on what to look for.

We leave dry recitations of facts and dates to the history books. We went after the historical texture of the region. And that often took us to offbeat tracks that helped us understand the ultimate American experience.

While researching Cape Cod, for instance, we found out that the Indians were the first American whalers.

Their technique was based on the observation that the trusting whales swam close to shore. They surrounded the whales with boats and splashed their oars, driving the whales to shore so that they could be easily killed.

We were surprised to learn that Cape Cod may have been discovered by a Viking or by Basque fishermen.

Off Martha's Vineyard, we came across an island called No Man's Land. On this island is a boulder that bears the date 1004 in eroded marks, presumably from an ancient visitor.

You may be confused when you hear Vineyarders (that's what the locals call themselves on Martha's Vineyard) speak of towns being Up-Island or Down-Island. That's not what you think, but we'll explain it. We'll also tell you about the town where no liquor is sold, where to find one of the oldest carousels in America, where to see intricate, rainbow-colored cottages, and how a street got its name because a resident bought a piano.

W e were fascinated by the lore of Nantucket. One favorite story involves the formation of the island. It seems that an Indian giant knocked his pipe ashes into the sea, causing Nantucket to rise from the sea. To give you an idea of the giant's size, he was so big that he snacked on whole roasted whales.

But Nantucket's history was not always so colorful. The somber lifestyle of the Quakers left its mark forever on the island. In fact, you'll learn why some of the island's names are still influenced by the frugality of the Quakers.

You can't talk about Nantucket without mentioning whales. And our research took us to the tropical Pacific Ocean origins of one of Nantucket's leading sea stories, "Moby Dick."

In order to put it all in perspective, we added wonderful old photographs and images of this historic mother lode.

"Cape Cod's Cooking Secrets" is an extraordinary book. We have a lot to share with you. Discover the secrets.

Watercress

Lemon Balm

Rosemary

Tansy

The Best Restaurants

Cape Cod

Martha's Vineyard

Nantucket

Cape Cod and the Islands

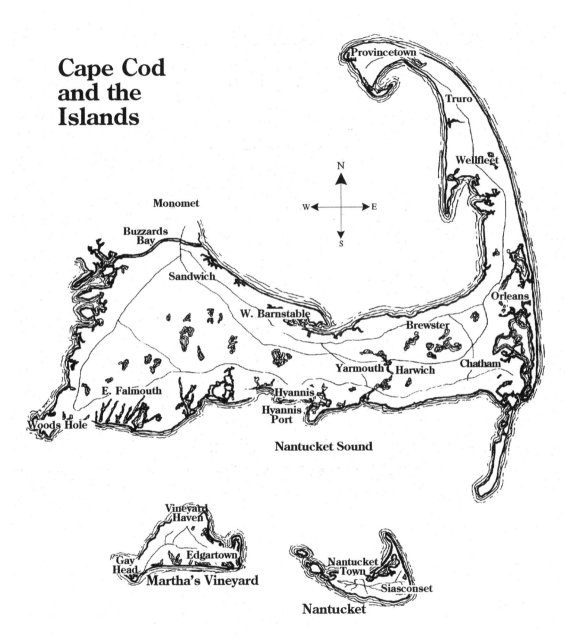

Provincetown

Truro

Wellfleet

Monomet

Buzzards Bay

Sandwich

W. Barnstable

Orleans

Brewster

Chatham

Yarmouth   Harwich

E. Falmouth

Hyannis

Hyannis Port

Woods Hole

Nantucket Sound

Vineyard Haven

Edgartown

Gay Head

Martha's Vineyard

Nantucket Town

Siasconset

Nantucket

Recipe Index

Breakfast

Appetizers

Final Temptations

Favorite Restaurant Recipes

AESOP'S TABLES

Menu for Four   30

CORN AND SHRIMP FRITTERS
ROASTED GARLIC CHOWDER
PROSCIUTTO STUFFED VEAL ROULADE
MACADAMIA FUDGE TART

AMERICAN SEASONS

Menu for Four   150

LOBSTER & WILD MUSHROOM PANCAKE
GRILLED VENISON IN SMOKED BARBECUE SAUCE

ANDREA'S

Menu for Four   114

CLAMS CASINO
LINGUINE PICANTE
LOBSTER FRA DIAVOLO

ANTHONY'S CUMMAQUID INN

Menu for Four   36

BOUILLABAISSE
BAKED STUFFED LOBSTER
INDIAN PUDDING

BOARDING HOUSE

Menu for Six   154

LACQUERED SHRIMP
WITH THAI PESTO NOODLES
ROASTED SALMON IN BUERRE ROUGE
CHOCOLATE BOURBON TERRINE

CAFÉ ELIZABETH

Menu for Four   40

GREENS WITH VINAIGRETTE
LES BLINIS AU CAVIAR
FROZEN RASPBERRY VODKA

CAPTAIN LINNELL HOUSE

Menu for Four   44

OYSTERS & VEGETABLES
IN CHAMPAGNE GINGER
ROAST PORK TENDERLOIN
WHITE CHOCOLATE MOUSSE,
DARK CHOCOLATE SAUCE

CIELO GALLERY-CAFÉ

Menu for Six   48

CAULIFLOWER CARAWAY SOUP
TOMATO FETTUCCINE, SHRIMP AND SCALLOPS
FILET OF SALMON IN PUFF PASTRY

THE CHANTICLEER

Menu for Four   160

CREAM OF ASPARAGUS SOUP
CHICKEN STUFFED WITH HERBS
CHOCOLATE DECADENCE WITH ESPRESSO SAUCE

CHATHAM BARS INN

Menu for Four   52

CREAM OF CHERVIL SOUP
LOBSTER AND FAVA BEAN SALAD
BANANA SOUFFLÉ

CHILLINGSWORTH

Menu for Four   56

OYSTERS AND SPINACH IN PUFF PASTRY
TWO MELON SOUP, CHAMPAGNE & MINT
LOBSTER, COGNAC CREAM

CHRISTIAN'S RESTAURANT

Menu for Eight   60

FRESH MAINE CRABCAKES
ROAST DUCK WITH PEAR AVOCADO SAUCE
COCONUT RUM CARAMEL CUSTARD
WITH ROASTED BANANA SAUCE

CLUB CAR

Menu for Four   164

SQUID WITH HOT ASIAN SPICES
SWEETBREADS GRAND MARNIER WITH GINGER
CHOCOLATE ALMOND MACAROONS

COONAMESSETT INN

Menu for Eight   64

LOBSTER CAKES WITH TOMATO COULIS
SALMON IN A CHARDONNAY MUSSEL CREAM

DAN'L WEBSTER INN

Menu for Four   68

SMOKED DUCKLING SALAD
MACADAMIA CASHEW CRUSTED STRIPED BASS
PINEAPPLE MASCARPONE VELVET

THE FLUME

Menu for Six   72

ESCALLOPED OYSTERS
ATLANTIC SALMON WITH EGG SAUCE
APPLE BROWN BETTY

THE GALLEY ON CLIFFSIDE BEACH

Menu for Six   168

CALAMARI SALAD
PAELLA
PEARS IN RASPBERRY SYRUP

HARBOR POINT

Menu for Two   76

DEVILS ON HORSEBACK
ASPARAGUS ARTICHOKE SALAD
YELLOWFIN TUNA CAPE CODDER

INDIA HOUSE

Menu for Four   172

STUFFED CALAMARI IN PESTO CREAM SAUCE
PECAN CASHEW GLAZED SWORDFISH
COFFEE ICE CREAM TRUFFLES
WITH HAZELNUTS

JARED COFFIN HOUSE

Menu for Eight   176

NANTUCKET BLUE SALAD
LOBSTER BISQUE
BAY SCALLOPS ON THE HALF SHELL

L'ÉTOILE

Menu for Four   118

OYSTER AND SPINACH CUSTARD
FOIE GRAS MANGO AND RASPBERRIES
WHITE CHOCOLATE RASPBERRY TART

LAMBERT'S COVE COUNTRY INN & RESTAURANT

SHRIMP, SCALLOPS, SAUSAGE STEW
SWORDFISH, MANGOS AND SWEET PEPPERS
VANILLA MOUSSE, FRESH RASPBERRIES
& BLACKBERRIES

LE LANGUEDOC

SOFT SHELL CRAB
OYSTER AND BRIE SOUP
SALAD, HERBAL VINAIGRETTE

NAPI'S

EMPRESS CAPS
VEGETABLE CURRY
CARROT CAKE

THE OUTERMOST INN

MARINATED MUSSELS
SEAFOOD STUFFED SOLE
BROWNIE CHEESECAKE

THE OYSTER BAR

OYSTER FRITTERS, REMOULADE SAUCE
SPLIT PEA SOUP WITH DARK RUM
PASTA WITH CILANTRO PESTO
ROSEMARY & GARLIC POTATOES
RATATOUILLE
TENDERLOIN WITH ROQUEFORT, GARLIC CREAM

THE PADDOCK

Menu for Two   **84**

CIOPPINO
SWORDFISH AU POIVRE
CHICKEN BREAST WITH ARTICHOKES & SHRIMP

POPPONESSET INN

Menu for Eight   **88**

NEW ENGLAND CLAM CHOWDER
LINGUINE WITH SALMON,
SCALLOPS CARBONARA
CHICKEN NANTUCKET

THE RED PHEASANT INN

Menu for Eight   **92**

TUNA WITH HONEY WASABI VINAIGRETTE
BRAISED PHEASANT IN BEAUJOLAIS
LINZER TORTE

THE REGATTA OF COTUIT

Menu for Four   **96**

ACORN SQUASH BISQUE
ROASTED STUFFED QUAIL, SAUCE MADEIRA
CHOCOLATE STRAWBERRIES

THE REGATTA OF FALMOUTH

Menu for Four   **100**

VEGETABLE RAVIOLIS
NEW ENGLAND SEA SCALLOP BISQUE
SOFT SHELL CRAB, RED PEPPER VINAIGRETTE
CHOCOLATE SEDUCTION CAKE

Cape Cod

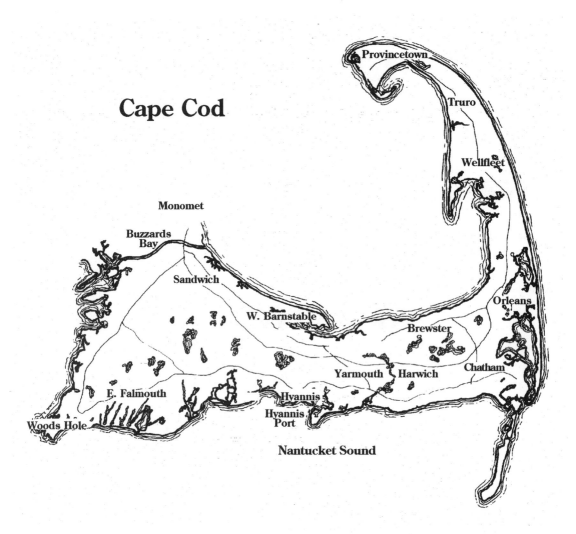

Think of Cape Cod as an outstretched arm, bent at the elbow, with the fist pointed back toward the mainland.

It is surrounded by water: the Atlantic to the east, Cape Cod Bay tucked in the crook of the arm to the west, Nantucket Sound to the south and separated from the mainland by the Cape Cod Canal.

The Cape is about 65 miles long and from 1 to 20 miles wide. It contains 15 towns, each broken up into villages, and has a permanent population of about 150,000, and about 500,000 during the season.

The portion abutting the mainland (where the biceps would be) is called the Upper Cape and contains the towns of Bourne, Falmouth, Mashpee and Sandwich, along with the Massachusetts Military Reservation, the Shawme-Crowell State Forest, and Woods Hole, the famed marine biology research center.

The central portion of the Cape, known as the Mid-Cape, extends to the elbow. It contains Barnstable, the largest town, plus the commercial center of Hyannis, and Hyannis Port, famed as the site of the Kennedy Compound.

The least developed portion of the Cape is known as the Lower Cape, which extends from the elbow to the fist. It contains the town of Chatham, the Monomoy National Wildlife Refuge (two islands set aside as an Audubon bird sanctuary), Nickerson State Park with its camping facilities, the expansive beaches, woods, swamps and visitors centers of the Cape Cod National Seashore, the towns of Wellfleet and Truro and ending in the fishing village of Provincetown.

The destiny of the Cape always has been bound to the sea. The first residents were the Wampanoag tribe, which numbered about 30,000 people. They figured out how to coax whales onto the beach—by surrounding them with boats and raising a commotion in order to drive the trusting whales to shore. They also devised methods to process the whales' blubber.

An Englishman, Bartholomew Gosnold, is generally credited as the first European to find Cape Cod, although some historians believe that the Viking Thorwald was shipwrecked there in 1004 and that he was followed by Basque fishermen. In any event, Gosnold named the Cape

CAPE COD: Bound to the Sea

❖

in honor of the great quantities of cod his men caught. But Goswald did not settle there.

Neither did Samuel de Champlain, the explorer and geographer for the king of France. He visited in 1605 and 1606, and ended up warring with the resident Wampanoags, with many deaths on both sides.

Settlement came with the Pilgrims, who sailed from England on the Mayflower in 1620. Actually, they were looking for some land that had been granted them by the Virginia Company. But after more than two months at sea, the 101 Pilgrims spotted Provincetown on November 21, 1620. They were far north of their intended destination, but the arduous journey and the approach of winter persuaded them to put ashore.

But first they made a little history by drawing up the Mayflower Compact, the first document establishing self-rule in America.

For several weeks, they sent a party ashore under the leadership of Capt. Miles Standish (you'll remember him from Pilgrim lore) to search for a proper settlement. They finally decided to establish a colony at Plymouth, on the mainland.

The wild new continent must have seemed overwhelming to the new settlers. They had left Elizabethan England just four years after Shakespeare's death. Some came to find refuge from religious persecution, some came for trade, many more came to experience the independence that comes from owning land.

Their first basic needs were food and shelter. Fishing and hunting were easy enough, but they knew that farming had to be the mainstay of their new communities. They had brought with them the complicated methods that had been developed for centuries in England. But in the forest of the new land they met people who had developed a simple agriculture suited to the needs of forest tribes. The settlers learned the new methods.

William Bradford, governor of the Plymouth colony, wrote of the Pilgrims emerging from their first terrible winter: "They (as many as were able) began to plant their corn in which servise Squanto stood them in great stead, showing them both the manner how to set, it and after how to dress and tend it... Some English seed they sew, as wheat and peas, but came to no good, either by the bad-

Friendly competition: The Pilgrims and the Indians match skills.

The storm-tossed Mayflower on its way to the new world

ness of the seed, or lateness of the season, or both, or some other defecte."

The early settlers found open spaces at the edge of the forest where they established farms. But more and more settlers came—and they all wanted open spaces for farming. Once again, they learned from the Indians: how to kill unwanted trees by girding them, then burning the dead trees and underbrush. This did establish open farmland, but it took an enormous toll on the forests.

The settlers' first homes were wigwams patterned after the Wampanoag homes. They were built of whatever materials were on hand: twigs, barks, hides, cornstalks and grasses. But it didn't take long for the settlers to start building homes more along European lines. Thus were born the steep-roofed saltbox and Cape Cod cottage that remain the architectural mainstays of the area.

The sea—always the sea—formed much of Cape Cod's history. At first, the settlers managed to live well from whales close to shore. In time, the whalers had to venture out further and further to reap the giants of the sea. The days of the New England whalers came into full flower. Many great fortunes were made. And many great legends were born.

Great fleets of whaling ships set out from Wellfleet, Truro and Provincetown, the only ports on the Cape deep enough to accommodate the ships.

And once the whalers had prospered and pioneered the concept of traveling great distances for a catch, the fishermen did likewise. Great quantities of seafood—cod and mackerel and halibut—were brought home. So, even after the whales had been depleted and the fabled days of the Cape Cod whalers waned, a great fishing industry prospered.

The fish trade, which grew to include lobsters, oysters and scallops, was always looking for new markets. One obstacle was the Cape itself, which cut off fishermen's access from Nantucket Sound to Cape Cod Bay and eventually to Boston. Dreamers began visualizing a canal as far back as the 17th century. The Cape Cod Canal, cutting the Cape from the mainland, but thereby allowing access to boats, was built in 1914. But it was narrow and winding and allowed only one-way traffic. The federal government bought the canal in 1928 and rebuilt it. Then in the

❖

The old railroad station in Cape Cod.

The Martha's Vineyard railroad station at Katama, Edgartown, circa 1875. The engine was named the "Active."

1930's three bridges were built and tourism—which has been encouraged since the 19th century—arrived with a flourish at Cape Cod.

However, the advent of tourism accentuated the need for protecting the magnificent coast from the ravages of overuse. The Cape Cod National Seashore was established in 1961. This insured that the Cape's entire eastern shoreline was protected for future generations. And, in order to keep a rein on over development, the Cape Cod Commission was established in 1990.

Today, tourism accounts for much of Cape Cod's income.

Artists are drawn to the pure light and simple lines of the Cape.

Writers flourish in the unspoiled beauty of the sandy shores.

Naturalists are drawn to the many species of birds.

Marine biologists are drawn by the abundance of sealife.

Visitors from all over the world are drawn by the picturesque villages, stately lighthouses, wealthy enclaves, powerful surf, gentle dunes, plentiful arts and crafts, ports with a taste of the old world, and historic inns.

And everyone is drawn by the exceptional food.

Vacationers gather in Oak Bluffs, circa 1915.

The Chatham Lighthouse

AESOP'S TABLES

NEW AMERICAN CUISINE
Main Street
Wellfleet Center
349-6450
Dinner 5:30PM–1AM
AVERAGE DINNER FOR TWO: $50

esop's Tables is a charming restaurant located in an 1800's Greek revival house built of ships' timbers. The restaurant has been a fixture in the center of the town of Wellfleet since 1965. Purchased in 1983 by Brian Dunne and his artist wife Kim Kettler, the restaurant has become a local institution.

The restaurant is run with energy and enthusiasm. Everything on the menu is made in-house. Among the starters frequently on the menu are corn and shrimp fritters with a Cajun remoulade, a colorful salad named Monet's Garden and nightly diversions, depending on the chef's whim. Fresh pasta selections are available in appetizer-sized portions as well. From the sea, a daily selection of fresh fish is either grilled or broiled and served with citrus butter or the chef's special sauce of the evening.

Aesop's Tables is a chocoholic's delight. Death by Chocolate, a dense mousse cake made from imported chocolate was voted Best Dessert on Cape Cod by Boston magazine. Other dessert offerings are native cranberries covered with a sweet pecan filling, served warm with vanilla ice cream and crêpes clementine—an orange custard tucked in lacy crêpes with a matching caramel sauce.

Aesop's Tables offers a warm, friendly atmosphere and exceptional food.

CHEF PETER RENNERT'S MENU FOR FOUR

Corn and Shrimp Fritters

Roasted Garlic Chowder

Prosciutto Stuffed Veal Roulade with Herb Goat's Cheese

Macadamia Fudge Tart (recipe by Caroline Freitas)

Corn and Shrimp Fritters

Combine all of the dry ingredients and set aside. Combine the beer, milk and egg and add the mixture slowly to the dry ingredients, mixing constantly. Stir until the batter is smooth. Add corn and green onions. Chop 20 shrimp and add to the mixture. Reserve 6 shrimp and split lengthwise. Refrigerate batter overnight.

Pour oil into a preheated, high-sided sauté pan. If possible, prop the pan up so the oil pools in the front of the pan. Spoon 4 Tbsps. of the fritter batter into the pool of oil. Press one of the split shrimp into the batter. When the first side is set, turn and brown the other side. Remove to a baking sheet. When all the fritters are done, place in a 350° oven for 10 minutes before serving. Serve warm.

Yield: 12–15 fritters
Preparation Time:
  30 Minutes
(note refrigeration time)

2½ cups all purpose flour
  2 tsps. baking powder
  3 tsps. salt
  3 tsps. black pepper
  1 tsp. red pepper flakes
    (optional)
1½ cups milk
  ½ bottle ale
    (Sam Adams, Bass)
  1 egg
1½ cups corn kernels
  2 green onions, chopped
 26 shrimp, cleaned,
    deveined
  4 Tbsps. oil

❖

Roasted Garlic Chowder

Serves 4
Preparation Time:
  One Hour
Pre-heat Oven to 350°

10 **heads of garlic, broken**
    into individual bulbs,
    unpeeled
¼ **cup oil**
 1 **medium onion, diced**
 3 **carrots, finely diced**
 3 **stalks celery, finely**
    diced
 2 **medium potatoes,**
    ¼" dice
 2 **tsps. dried thyme**
 2 **bay leaves**
 4 **qts. chicken stock**
    Salt and pepper to taste

Toss the garlic in oil and place on a baking sheet. Place in a 350° oven for 20 minutes or until the garlic is soft. Remove from baking sheet, cool and peel. Set aside.

Sauté the onion, carrots, celery, potatoes, thyme and bay leaves in a large stock pot. When the onions begin to brown, add the stock. Allow this to simmer until the potatoes are soft.

While the vegetables are cooking, process half the roasted garlic into paste, adding liquid from the soup pot if necessary. Roughly chop the remaining garlic. Add all the garlic to the soup. The puréed garlic will act as at thickener. Season with salt and pepper.

❖

Prosciutto Stuffed Veal Roulades

Pound veal medallions as thin as possible without tearing then season with salt and pepper. Combine the goat cheese with herbs and season with salt and pepper. Be careful of the salt, some cheeses are salty to begin with.

Cover the medallions with a slice of Prosciutto and then spread a layer of cheese mixture. Tightly roll the medallion and fasten the loose end with toothpicks if necessary.

Dredge the roulade in the flour, pat off the excess. Dunk it in the egg wash, and dredge it in the bread crumbs. Set it aside.

Heat oil in a sauté pan and brown the roulade on all sides. Finish in a 450° oven for 8 to 12 minutes until medium rare.

For the sauce, sauté the shallots in olive oil until translucent. Add the tomatoes, toss and add a splash of white wine. Cook for 2 minutes and then add basil, salt and pepper to taste.

Serve immediately over the roulade.

Trade Secret: Linguini is a great accompaniment with this dish.

Serves 4
Preparation Time:
   45 Minutes
Pre-heat oven to 450°

8 oz. veal loin cut into
   2 oz. medallions
4 oz. goat cheese
4 Tbsps. finely chopped
   fresh herbs (parsley, basil,
   thyme, oregano)
4 slices Prosciutto, cut very
   thin
1 cup flour
2 eggs beaten with 2 Tbsps.
   water
1 cup plain fresh bread
   crumbs
   Olive oil
1 Tbsp. diced shallot
4 ripe plum tomatoes,
   chopped
   White wine
2 Tbsps. basil, coarsely
   chopped
   Salt and pepper to taste

Macadamia Fudge Tart

Yields: Two 11″ tarts
Preparation Time:
  One Hour

1½ cups sugar
  4 Tbsps. light corn syrup
  8 Tbsps. (1 stick) butter
  1 cup heavy cream
  1 lb. macadamia nuts,
    toasted
    Two 11″ tart shells,
    pre-baked
    Chocolate ganache,
    recipe follows

Combine the sugar and corn syrup in a medium pot and cook on medium high heat until deep caramel in color. Add the butter a piece at a time, stirring while adding. Add the cream and cook until smooth. Remove from heat and stir in the nuts.

Divide the mixture while warm between the two tart shells and spread evenly. Chill well.

❖

Chocolate Ganache

Chop the chocolate and melt in a double boiler. Heat the cream and butter and pour into the chocolate while melting. Remove from heat and mix well until smooth and shiny.

Once the tarts and ganache are cool, ladle the filling into the tarts and spread evenly into a thin layer. Set aside.

Chill the remaining ganache so it is stiff enough to pipe through a pastry bag.

Before serving, finish the tarts by piping small rosettes of ganache around the border of each tart.

12 oz. dark chocolate
1 cup heavy cream
3 Tbsps. butter

ANTHONY'S CUMMAQUID INN

NEW ENGLAND CUISINE
Route 6A
Yarmouth Port
362-4501
Dinner 6PM–10PM
AVERAGE DINNER FOR TWO: $60

Formerly a stately old home, Anthony's Cummaquid Inn retains much of its original splendor. The original home was located in a glorious setting surrounded by magnificent grounds. The spacious main dining room, built on an elevation, overlooks a pond and offers a beautiful view of Cape Cod. Decorated with colonial furnishings, the restaurant is a charming testament to a bygone era.

The menu is traditionally New England with a spattering of international cuisine. New England mainstays like Anthony Athanas' bouillabaisse and lobster bisque are featured on the menu. Entrées such as the baked stuffed lobster à la Hawthorne and a stuffed filet of sole, moist and flaky, lets guests sample even more of the Atlantic's bounty. Besides seafood, an impressive selection of beef and steaks is available, like the entrée of roast beef au jus. An impressive wine list complements the restaurant's fine cuisine.

ANTHONY ATHANAS' MENU FOR FOUR

Bouillabaisse

Baked Stuffed Lobster

Indian Pudding

Bouillabaisse

emove and crack the lobster claws. Remove the tails and halve them lengthwise. Discard the bodies, but reserve the tails and claws.

Sauté the leeks, onion and garlic in olive oil. Add the wine, Pernod, mustard, saffron, tomatoes and tomato paste and the fish stock. Add white pepper to taste and simmer, uncovered, over low heat for one hour.

Add the salmon or tuna, swordfish, cod, mussels, shrimp and scallops. Cover and cook until the clams open and the filets are cooked through, about 10 minutes.

To serve, place an assortment of fish and shellfish in large individual bowls; then ladle the vegetables and soup over the fish.

Serves 4
Preparation Time:
   1½ Hours

   2 lobsters, boiled or
      steamed, 1½ lbs. each
   2 leeks, chopped
   1 onion, diced
   2 garlic cloves, diced
   ¼ cup olive oil
   1 cup white wine
   ¼ cup Pernod
   1 Tbsp. Dijon mustard
   1 tsp. saffron
   1 can (28 oz.) plum
      tomatoes, drained,
      coarsely chopped
   2 Tbsps. tomato paste
   8 cups fish stock
      White pepper to taste
   ½ lb. salmon or tuna
   ½ lb. swordfish
   ½ lb. cod
   2 dozen mussels
   2 dozen shrimp
   2 dozen scallops

Baked Stuffed Lobster

Serves 4
Preparation Time:
  30 Minutes
Pre-heat oven to 350°

4 lobsters
1 cup lobster meat, cooked,
   chopped
8 Tbsps. butter (1 stick),
   melted
4 cups bread crumbs
4 Tbsps. parsley
4 Tbsps. shallots, chopped
   Drawn butter
   Lemon wedges

A reasonably humane way to kill a lobster is to grasp it by the tail to steady it, and then jab the tip of a large, sharp knife between the eyes—this will kill it instantly. Then split each lobster in half under the belly, leaving the shell whole.

In a mixing bowl combine the cooked lobster meat with the melted butter. Add the bread crumbs, parsley and shallots. Stuff each lobster with 4 Tbsps. of the bread crumb mixture.

Cover and bake 10 to 12 minutes for a medium lobster or 15 to 20 minutes for a large lobster. Bake uncovered for the last 5 minutes to brown the stuffing.

If the tail curls, put weight on it during cooking.

Serve with drawn butter and lemon wedges.

Indian Pudding

In a double boiler, heat the milk until it simmers gently. Add the cornmeal and granulated sugar.

Beat the eggs, brown sugar, molasses and spices together in a large mixing bowl. Add this mixture to the heated milk.

Place the pudding in a loaf pan and add the raisins. Set the loaf pan in a larger pan with about one inch of water in it.

Bake at 400° for 1½ hours or until the pudding is firm and lightly browned.

Serves 8
Preparation Time:
  2 Hours
Pre-heat oven to 400°

  1 qt. whole milk
 ½ cup cornmeal
 ½ cup granulated sugar
  7 eggs
 ¼ cup packed brown sugar
 ⅓ cup molasses
 ½ tsp. cinnamon
 ½ tsp. ginger
 ½ tsp. nutmeg
    Dash of salt
  1 cup raisins

CAFÉ ELIZABETH

FRENCH CUISINE
31 Sea Street
Harwich Port
432-1147
Dinner 6PM–10PM
AVERAGE DINNER FOR TWO: $80

O riginally a sea captain's home, this charming French country restaurant is situated a few blocks from the ocean. You enter Café Elizabeth through a brightly flowered garden path. Once inside, you will see a number of intimate dining areas beautifully decorated with French antique furnishings, white lace curtains, velvet upholstery and French paintings.

The head chef, Paul Nebbia and his wife, Marguerite, came to Cape Cod from Washington, D.C., following an impressive career that included the Restaurant Laurent in Paris, the prestigious Connaught Hotel in London, the Hotel Ritz in Lisbon, and the Rive Gauche in Georgetown.

The menu they have devised features classic French cuisine in the grand style—elegant but relaxed. Menu highlights are breast of chicken in a curry sauce with raisins, almonds and apples or La Palette du Chef—an assortment of four medallions: lobster with lobster sauce, veal with wild mushrooms, lamb with fresh tarragon, and filet of beef with Béarnaise sauce. Appetizers include black wheat pancakes filled with sour cream, fresh salmon caviar with a glass of homemade frozen cranberry vodka or spicy lamb sausage served with kidney beans.

Marguerite's trademark desserts include Les Truffles au Chocolat de Marguerite—the darkest Belgian chocolates and Grand Marnier marry to make a sinful chocolate truffle served on a bed of fresh whipped cream with chocolate sauce and roasted almonds.

CHEF PAUL FRANÇOIS NEBBIA'S MENU FOR FOUR

Greens with Vinaigrette

Les Blinis au Caviar

Frozen Raspberry Vodka

Greens with Vinaigrette

 Finely grind the garlic cloves and the shallots. Add salt and pepper and continue to grind. The mixture will look like a paste by the time you finish.

Add the mustard, vinegar, and oil. Mix very well.

Put the vinaigrette in a closed jar and store in the refrigerator.

Shake jar vigorously before using on your favorite salad greens.

Serves 6
Yields: ¾ cup dressing
Preparation Time:
**   10 Minutes**
(note refrigeration time)

   3 **garlic cloves**
   1 **shallot**
   ½ **tsp. salt**
   ¼ **tsp. ground pepper**
   1 **tsp. Dijon mustard**
   4 **Tbsps. wine vinegar**
   8 **Tbsps. olive oil**
   1 **lb. mixed salad greens**

Blinis with Caviar

Serves 6
Preparation Time:
  30 Minutes

  1 **cup whole wheat flour**
  4 **eggs**
     Pinch of salt
  ½ **cup warm milk**
  ½ **cup beer, room**
     temperature
  1½ **cups sour cream**
  12 **oz. salmon roe caviar**
  4 **Tbsps. butter**

 n a medium-size mixing bowl, mix together the flour, eggs and salt. Add warm milk and whisk until smooth. Add beer and mix.

Heat a griddle over medium-high heat, then butter it lightly. Gently drop the batter by heaping tablespoons, about 2 Tbsps.

Cook until the bottoms are golden and bubbles are popping on the surface, about 1 minute. Turn, and cook 1 minute on the other side. Repeat, using up all the batter, which will yield twelve 6″ pancakes.

Fill each warm pancake with a heaping tablespoon of sour cream. Top with one ounce of fresh salmon roe caviar. Gently fold the blini over once.

Pour a teaspoon of melted butter over the entire pancake and serve immediately on a warm plate.

Trade Secret: A glass of homemade frozen raspberry vodka is a wonderful accompaniment. Recipe follows.

Frozen Raspberry Vodka

O ne by one, drop the raspberries into an empty vodka bottle. Fill with your favorite vodka, leaving room enough for the mixture to expand when you freeze it later. Cap it.

Keep at room temperature for two weeks. Turn the bottle upside down a few times to make sure the color of the berries blends nicely with the vodka. Place the bottle in the freezer for 24 hours before drinking.

When it's ready, the vodka should have the consistency of thick syrup, the color will be pale pink and the flavor very delicate.

For an impressive show, place the frozen bottle in a plastic bucket twice as large as the bottle. Cover the bottle with water, leaving 4" at the top to allow for the ice to expand. Place rose petals or fresh raspberries in the water. Put the bucket in the freezer. When the ice is hard, run the bucket under warm water to remove it, and voila!—your own ice sculpture from which to serve your raspberry vodka.

Yield: 1 liter bottle
Preparation Time:
  5 Minutes
(note refrigeration time)

2 **cups very ripe, red**
  raspberries
1 **liter vodka**

❖

THE CAPTAIN LINNELL HOUSE

CLASSIC AMERICAN CUISINE
137 Skaket Beach Road
Orleans
255-3400
Dinner 5PM–9PM
Sunday Brunch 11AM–2PM
AVERAGE DINNER FOR TWO: $50–$60

T he Captain Linnell House is a gracious and historic sea captain's mansion. This neo-classic villa was built amid beautiful pastoral surroundings in 1840 by Captain Ebenezer Linnell as a wedding present for his bride. The grounds, which include a gazebo, fountains, lawns and historic 150-year-old European linden tree, wrap the building in a special aura of another era. Now owned and operated by Chef Bill Conway and his family, this magnificent building has been lovingly restored with great attention to detail.

Inside is a series of cozy dining rooms with exposed beams, a Normandy fireplace and rose chintz drapes framing windows overlooking the garden. The printed dinner menu is supplemented by handwritten nightly specials that may include roast tenderloin of beef wrapped with a paté of veal, served with a red wine peppercorn sauce, a grilled boneless chicken breast with a Pommery mustard sauce and cranberry pear chutney or scrod, shrimp and Maine crab in parchment with a lemon-lime vermouth sauce.

The Captain Linnell House is a little off the beaten path but well worth looking for.

CHEF WILLIAM CONWAY'S MENU FOR FOUR

Linnell Oysters

Roast Pork Tenderloin with Caramelized Onions and Maple Demi-Glaze

White Chocolate Mousse with Dark Chocolate Sauce

Linnell Oysters

n a sauté pan melt butter and add the shallots, ginger, oysters, and julienne vegetables. Sauté for 2 minutes.

Flambé with Pernod. Add champagne.

Remove oysters and vegetables from liquid. Don't overcook. Reduce champagne by half. Add heavy cream and reduce until it coats the back of a spoon. Add the oysters and vegetables to warm.

Split puff pastry triangles in half and brush with beaten egg. Bake for 15 minutes or until brown.

Top pastry with oysters and vegetables. Serve warm.

Serves 4
Preparation Time:
 45 Minutes
Pre-heat oven to 350°

32 oysters, shucked,
 reserve all liquid
 2 Tbsps. butter
 1 Tbsp. shallots, chopped
 1 tsp. fresh ginger, grated
 1 leek, only the white
 part, julienne
 1 carrot, julienne
 1 small zucchini, julienne,
 2 Tbsps. Pernod
 1 cup champagne
 2 cups heavy cream
 Pinch of salt
 4 puff pastry triangles
 (split and brush with
 egg and score with knife
 before baking)

Roast Pork Tenderloin with Caramelized Onions and Maple Demi-Glaze

Serves 4
Preparation Time:
 45 Minutes
Pre-heat Oven to 400°

2 pork tenderloins,
  approximately 2 lbs.
  total
  Flour for dredging
½ cup olive oil
1 large onion, julienne
3 cups veal or beef stock
½ cup maple syrup
6 shiitake mushrooms,
  sliced
¼ cup bourbon
½ cup white wine vinegar
1 tsp. shallots, chopped
1 stick butter

Trim any fat or membranes from pork. Dredge lightly in flour with a pinch of salt.

Place 4 Tbsps. olive oil in a sauté pan. Brown the meat and place in a shallow roasting pan. Roast for 20 minutes or until internal temperature is 165° or juices run clear.

While pork is roasting, heat 3 Tbsps. olive oil in a sauté pan with the onion over medium heat. Add 1 cup stock to the onions. Stir frequently and cook for 7 to 10 minutes or until the onions take on a rich brown, caramelized look. Add the sliced mushrooms and sauté lightly.

Pour the bourbon over the onion mixture and finish with maple syrup and remaining stock. Cook until liquid becomes syrupy.

Remove pork from oven and cut across grain.

To serve, pour a pool of the maple demi-glaze onto individual dinner plates. Fan the pork slices over the sauce.

❖

White Chocolate Mousse with Dark Chocolate Sauce

Break the white chocolate into chunks and place them with the butter in the top of a double boiler over simmering water. Over low heat, combine the chocolate and butter, stirring constantly, until melted. Whisk in the egg yolks one at a time. Set aside and cool to lukewarm.

In a separate bowl, beat the egg whites with sugar to soft peaks and combine with the chocolate mixture. Refrigerate overnight.

Before serving, whip cream about half way. Add the cold mousse and whip until stiff. Break the semi-sweet chocolate into chunks and place them in the top of a double boiler over simmering water. Heat until melted, stirring occasionally. Add the cream, milk and vanilla.

To serve, spoon a pool of chocolate sauce onto individual plates. Top with white chocolate mousse. Dust with powdered sugar. Garnish with fresh mint leaves.

Serves 4
Preparation Time:
  45 Minutes
(note refrigeration time)
Pre-heat oven to 425°

  2 **lbs. white chocolate,**
     chopped
  2 **sticks of butter cut into**
     small pieces
 12 **eggs, separated**
  ½ **cup sugar**
  1 **pint heavy cream,**
     whipped
1½ **lbs. semi-sweet**
     chocolate
  2 **cups heavy cream**
  1 **cup milk**
  3 **Tbsps. vanilla extract**
     Powdered sugar
     Mint leaves, garnish

❖

CIELO GALLERY-CAFÉ

NEW AMERICAN CUISINE
East Main Street
Wellfleet
349-2108
Lunch Noon–2PM
Dinner 8PM seating, by reservation only.
AVERAGE DINNER FOR TWO: $80

T he restaurant's name, Cielo, is Italian for "Heaven" and reflects the experience of dining at the restaurant. Rated by Boston Magazine as one of the top dining establishments on Cape Cod, the restaurant offers a splendid view of the natural surroundings from its glass enclosed dining room along with sumptuous meals. Also serving as an art gallery, local artists have their creations on display in the 100-year-old "salt-box" house.

Chef John Burns and his wife, Martha Zschock, combine their culinary and artistic talents to bring the perfect combination of food and art to their guests. The guests are even welcome in the kitchen to chat and see the evening's meals.

A traditional lunch menu has such enticing items as Grilled Fontina, Basil and Prosciutto on thick sourdough bread, Chicken Chipolte Ravioli, and a Spinach and Feta Ravioli.

Dinner is unique with entrées like Salmon in Puff Pastry, homemade Gorgonzola Walnut Ravioli, and Scallop Bisque. Delicious endings include such tempting desserts as Chocolate Torte with Brandy Crème Anglaise or a fresh Peach Tart with whipped cream.

CHEF JOHN BURNS' MENU FOR SIX

Cauliflower Caraway Soup

Tomato Fettuccine with Shrimp and Scallops

Filet of Salmon, Spinach and Tomato in Puff Pastry

Cauliflower-Caraway Soup

Melt butter in a stock pot. Add onions and garlic and sauté over medium heat until onions are translucent. Add chicken stock, wine, potatoes, cauliflower, caraway seeds, salt and pepper. Simmer on low heat for 30–35 minutes. Purée the soup in a blender or food processor fitted with a steel blade until smooth. If necessary, adjust consistency with more wine and/or stock. Adjust seasoning.

Garnish with freshly chopped chives.

Serves 6
Preparation Time:
   25 Minutes

8 **Tbsps. (1 stick) butter**
2 **medium onion, chopped**
2 **garlic cloves, minced**
1 **cup dry white wine**
6 **cups chicken stock**
1 **large potato, peeled, diced**
1 **head cauliflower, trimmed**
1 **tsp. caraway seeds**
   Salt and pepper to taste
1 **Tbsp. fresh chives, chopped**

❖

Tomato Fettuccine with Shrimp and Scallops

Serves 6
Preparation Time:
  30 Minutes

 1 **medium onion,**
   chopped
 2 **garlic cloves, minced**
 4 **Tbsps. olive oil**
 1 **cup dry white wine**
 2 **tsps. fish bouillon base**
¾ **cup mushrooms, thinly**
   sliced
 2 **cups heavy cream**
¼ **cup Parmesan cheese,**
   finely grated
⅓ **cup fresh parsley,**
   chopped
12 **large shrimp, peeled**
   and deveined
¾ **lb. bay scallops**
 4 **Italian plum tomatoes,**
   peeled, seeded,
   chopped
   Salt and pepper to taste
 1 **lb. tomato fettuccine**
   Parsley, garnish
   Parmesan cheese

 n a large sauce pan, sauté the onions and garlic in olive oil and cook until translucent. Whisk in wine and fish base and bring to a boil.

Lower heat to a simmer, add the mushrooms, and reduce the liquid by half. Add the heavy cream and continue to simmer on low heat for about 10 to 15 minutes, or until the sauce is slightly thickened and reduced. Whisk in the Parmesan cheese and parsley and cook one minute longer.

Bring a large saucepan of salted water to a boil. Add shrimp and scallops. Cook for one minute, then drain immediately.

To the sauce, add the shrimp, scallops, tomatoes, salt and pepper to taste. Stir to combine.

Serve over tomato fettuccine and garnish with freshly chopped parsley and finely grated parmesan cheese.

Salmon, Spinach and Tomato in Puff Pastry

T haw the pastry according to the directions on the package.

Roll out one sheet of pastry to ⅛" thick. Place one filet on the lower third of the pastry. Drizzle 1 Tbsp. each of the wine and lemon juice on the filet and season with salt and pepper. Sprinkle half of the shallots and garlic evenly over the filet.

Place half of the tomatoes on top of the filet, overlapping them slightly. Arrange half of the spinach over the tomatoes. Carefully roll the filet jelly-roll fashion. Trim both ends of excess pastry and crimp to enclose.

Place on a greased baking sheet, seam side down, so that the tomatoes and spinach are on the top.

Brush with egg wash and melted butter. Repeat with second filet. Bake for 20 minutes or until the pastry is golden brown.

Slice each filet diagonally into three servings.

Serves 6
Preparation Time:
  45 Minutes
Pre-heat oven to 400°

2 sheets frozen puff pastry
2 salmon filets, 1 lb. each, skinned
2 Tbsps. dry white wine
2 Tbsps. fresh lemon juice
  Salt and pepper to taste
4 shallots, minced
3 garlic cloves, minced
3 Italian plum tomatoes, sliced medium thick
1 cup fresh spinach, stems removed
1 egg, beaten
4 Tbsps. butter, melted

❖

CHATHAM BARS INN

CONTEMPORARY NEW ENGLAND CUISINE
Shore Road
Chatham
945-0096
Breakfast 6:30AM–8:30AM
Lunch Noon–2PM
Dinner 6:30PM–9:30PM
AVERAGE DINNER FOR TWO: $65

C hatham Bars Inn is a Cape Cod landmark and one of the last of America's grand oceanfront resorts. Built in 1914 as a hunting lodge by a wealthy Boston family, it has since become a year-round destination famous for gracious service, fine cuisine and unequaled natural beauty.

The main dining room, with its touch of formality and an unparalleled ocean view, serves elegant New England cuisine. The tavern at the inner bar has cozy, club-like surroundings and features a more casual menu. And, in summer, the beach house grill serves light luncheon fare and traditional New England clam and lobster bakes, right at the water's edge.

The inn's award-winning chef, Robert Trainor, describes his cooking as a "cross between French and New England," using local products whenever possible, from cheese to poultry. Entrees may include seafood minestrone with basil pesto, roast saddle of lamb, chanterelles and spinach perfumed with thyme, or veal sweetbreads braised with fava beans and pearl onions, in a lobster paprika sauce.

CHEF ROBERT TRAINOR'S MENU FOR FOUR

Cream of Chervil Soup

Lobster and Fava Bean Salad with Pancetta Mignonette

Banana Soufflé

Cream of Chervil Soup

lanch half of the chervil in two cups of salted water. Refresh under cold water and reserve the water.

Sweat the shallots, potato and remaining chervil along with the bay leaf and peppercorns in 4 Tbsps. butter. Add the Riesling and reduce by half. Add the chervil stock and chicken stock as well as the heavy cream. Reduce the soup until it becomes thick. Strain and reserve the potatoes.

Place soup, blanched chervil and potatoes in a blender. Blend until creamy and bright green in color. Add the crème fraîche. Season to taste and strain.

Garnish with a dollop of crème fraîche and fresh chervil leaves or American caviar.

Serves 4
Preparation Time:
45 Minutes

½ cup fresh chervil, chopped
4 Tbsps. shallots
1 medium-size potato, peeled, diced
2 garlic cloves, minced
1 bay leaf
1 Tbsp. white peppercorns
8 Tbsps. (1 stick) sweet butter
3 Tbsps. Riesling wine
1 cup chicken stock
2 cups heavy cream
2 Tbsps. crème fraîche
Salt, cayenne pepper, and nutmeg to taste
Caviar, optional

Lobster and Fava Bean Salad
with Pancetta Mignonette

Serves 4
Preparation Time:
  30 Minutes

  2 oz. pancetta, thinly
    sliced
  4 Tbsps. shallots, diced
  ½ cup champagne vinegar
    Black pepper, freshly
    ground
  2 Tbsps. fresh tarragon
    leaves
  2 lobsters, 1¾ lbs. each,
    poached, cleaned
  ½ cup fresh fava beans,
    blanched, peeled
  1 tomato
  1 head frisse lettuce

C hop the pancetta into ½" pieces. Sauté them in a heavy skillet over medium-low heat until just crisp, 10 minutes. Add the shallots and cook quickly. Drain on paper towels and set aside.

In a mixing bowl, combine the vinegar, pepper, and tarragon leaves. Add the pancetta and shallots. Adjust seasonings to taste and set aside.

Split each lobster tail in half and remove the vein. Reserve claw and knuckle meat for other uses.

In a large mixing bowl, combine the 4 lobster tail halves with the fava beans. Add 1 to 2 Tbsps. of the pancetta mixture, to taste. Set aside.

Peel and seed the tomato. Cut into wedges to use for garnish.

Arrange each lobster tail half with the fava beans in 4 chilled soup plates. Garnish with frisse and tomato wedges. Serve with the pancetta mignonette.

❖

Banana Soufflé

Peel the banana and pureé. Set aside.
Beat the egg whites and sugar with an electric mixer to soft peaks. Fold in the egg yolk, flour and scraped vanilla. Fold in the banana purée.

Butter four ramekins and sprinkle them with sugar. Arrange the prepared ramekins on a baking sheet and fill them with the soufflé mixture.

Bake until puffed, 8 minutes.

Sift confectioners sugar and cinnamon over the top and serve immediately.

Serves 4
Preparation Time:
   30 Minutes
Pre-heat oven to 400°

1 **over-ripe banana**
3 **egg whites**
¼ **cup sugar**
1 **egg yolk**
1½ **Tbsps. flour**
¼ **vanilla bean, scraped**
   Confectioners sugar,
   for dusting
   Cinnamon

CHILLINGSWORTH

FRENCH AMERICAN CUISINE
Route 6A
Brewster
896-3640
Dinner seating Tues.–Sun., 6:00PM, 6:30PM, 9:00PM, 9:30PM
Greenhouse Bar Tues.–Sun., 11:30AM–2:00PM
AVERAGE DINNER FOR TWO: $135–$160

Pairing classic French training with cutting-edge nouvelle cuisine, Robert (Nitzy) Rabin and his wife, Pat, a pastry expert, create award-winning dishes at Chillingsworth. The Rabins have been serving their innovative meals for more than 17 years at the three-century-old mansion in Brewster.

Guests dine by candlelight in any one of the five dining rooms at the restaurant. Each room is decorated in Louis XV antiques and reproductions and the restaurant has working fireplaces. A harpist gently plays in the background while guests dine.

The menu is composed by Chef Rabin daily and is a five-course prix fixe meal featuring such entrées as Venison with Celery Root Purée and Fried Pumpkin, or Grilled Poussin served with Raspberry Sauce and accompanied by fresh vegetables. A stunning entrée is the Grilled Loin of Veal with Saffron Rissotto, Garlic Custard and Wild Mushroom Sauce. As appetizers, fried mussels on top of a bed of mustard sauce and tiny cakes of crab and crayfish with a spicy, but mild, saffron sauce are two tempting choices.

Pat's creations—a flourless chocolate cake with English cream, or a Mango Crème Brûlée with Fresh Raspberries—are just two of the pastry expert's delicious finales.

CHEF ROBERT RABIN'S MENU FOR FOUR

Oysters and Spinach in Puff Pastry

Two Melon Soup with Champagne and Mint

Lobster with Spinach, French Beans & Basil in Cognac Cream

Oysters and Spinach in Puff Pastry

Remove the oysters from their shells by placing the oyster on a towel in the palm of your hand. Insert the tip of a knife between the shells and work the knife back and forth to carefully pry the shells apart. Cut from underneath to free the oyster from the shell. Set the oysters aside.

To prepare the sauce, combine the egg, lemon juice, and a pinch of salt and pepper in a food processor. With the processor running, slowly add the melted butter. When the butter has emulsified, stop the processor and taste for seasoning. Adjust salt and pepper and add more lemon juice to taste. Don't forget that the salmon roe may be slightly salty when it is added. Hold the sauce in a bain-marie over low heat, about 155°.

Gently poach the oysters in water and white wine.

While the oysters are poaching, sauté the spinach at a high temperature, adding a small amount of whole unsalted butter, some salt and pepper and a sprinkle of water.

Place the sautéed spinach in the bottom half of each pastry, add the heated asparagus spears, cover the spinach and the asparagus stems with the poached oysters.

In a separate bowl, mix the sauce with the minced chives and the salmon roe. Drizzle the sauce over the oysters. Place the puff pastry top over the oysters and serve.

Serves 4
Preparation Time:
  45 Minutes

20 oysters
 1 egg
¼ cup fresh lemon juice
   Salt and pepper
 1 cup (2 sticks) unsalted
   butter, melted
¼ cup white wine
 1 bunch spinach, cleaned
 4 thin asparagus spears,
   cut to 4½", blanched
   al dente
 3 Tbsps. chives, finely
   minced
 4 tsps. salmon roe
 4 puff pastries, 2½" × 4",
   baked in advance

Two Melon Soup with Champagne & Mint

Serves 4
Preparation Time:
  20 Minutes

  1 **medium cantaloupe**
  1 **medium honeydew**
  1 **cup champagne**
  2 **cups fresh orange juice**
¼ **cup fresh lime juice**
  1 **Tbsp. honey**
½ **cup heavy cream,**
    whipped
    Fresh mint leaves

 Peel and seed each melon. Cut melons in half. Mince one half of each melon and cut the other half into bite-size pieces.

Combine the larger pieces of melons with the orange juice, lime juice and honey, blending thoroughly. Add the minced melons and champagne to taste.

To serve, ladle the fruit into individual serving bowls and top with unsweetened whipped cream and fresh mint leaves as garnish.

Lobster with a Basil Cognac Cream

Poach or steam the lobsters until they are medium-rare, about 3 to 4 minutes. Cool and remove the meat from the shells, utilizing the two claws, the tail cut lengthwise. Save the knuckle meat and other lobster scraps, including the roe, for the sauce.

Place the lobster in a buttered baking dish. Add salt, pepper and white wine. Cover with parchment paper. Place in a warm oven for 6 to 8 minutes. The meat should "steam bake" until just hot, not overcooked.

In a sauté pan, melt the butter over a medium heat. Add the reserved lobster meat and cognac. Add the stock or white veal glaze and reduce. Add the heavy cream and bring to a boil. Add the chopped basil. Taste and adjust seasonings if necessary. Strain and place the sauce aside in a bain-marie if it won't be served immediately.

To serve, drape the basil cognac cream over the lobster.

Serves 4
Preparation Time:
  One Hour
Pre-heat oven to 350°

4 **lobsters, 1½ lbs. each**
  Salt and pepper
½ **cup white wine**
4 **Tbsps. butter**
½ **cup cognac**
12 **large basil leaves,**
  chopped
½ **cup heavy cream**
  Chicken stock or white
  veal glaze

❖

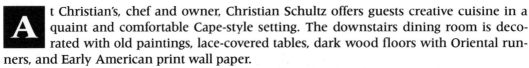

CHRISTIAN'S RESTAURANT

CLASSIC NEW ENGLAND CUISINE
443 Main Street
Chatham
945-3362
Lunch and Dinner 11:30AM–1AM
AVERAGE DINNER FOR TWO: $30

At Christian's, chef and owner, Christian Schultz offers guests creative cuisine in a quaint and comfortable Cape-style setting. The downstairs dining room is decorated with old paintings, lace-covered tables, dark wood floors with Oriental runners, and Early American print wall paper.

A library bar, located upstairs, offers a comfortable place for guests to enjoy a cocktail and meal inside or outside on the outdoor patio. The dark mahogany panels, old estate furniture and a bookshelf running along the ceiling give the room a homey and study-like feel.

Upstairs, guests can enjoy a menu divided into cinema theme sections. Previews include such items as Great Balls of Fire which are fiery crab and corn fritters served with a salsa sour cream, or La Dolce Vita, an antipasto plate filled with marinated and chilled vegetables, meats and cheeses served with toasted herb bread. Burgers named The Cagney and The Bogart are oversized grilled burgers served with onions, lettuce, tomatoes, fries and a plethora of toppings suggested by the star's name.

Dinner downstairs at Christian's is a more formal affair and is highlighted by such entrées as Seafood Jambalaya. This dish is made of lobster, shrimp and scallops simmered to perfection with mushrooms and scallions in a spicy tomato sauce served over rice and garnished with more fruits of the sea, mussels and clams. A crispy Roast Duck served with Ginger Peach Sauce, and fresh pasta tossed with olive oil and lemon pepper are just two more of the many delicious selections.

For appetizers, the raw bar serves littlenecks on the half shell, oysters and shrimp cocktails. Yukae, a Japanese appetizer, is a steak tartare, tossed with pine nuts and ponzu sauce and is served with fried won tons.

CHEF CHRISTIAN SCHULTZ'S MENU FOR EIGHT

Fresh Maine Crabcakes

Roast Duck with Pear and Avocado Sauce

Coconut Rum Caramel Custard with Roasted Banana Sauce

Maine Crabcakes

Mix all ingredients together in a bowl. Shape into 2 oz. cakes and sauté in clarified butter.
Serve with lemon butter.

Serves 8
Preparation Time:
   30 Minutes

1½ **lbs. crab, fresh Maine**
     red crab preferred
  1 **Tbsp. red pepper,**
     finely diced
  1 **Tbsp. green pepper,**
     finely diced
  1 **Tbsp. yellow pepper,**
     finely diced
  1 **Tbsp. parsley, finely**
     diced
  3 **Tbsps. onion, diced,**
     sautéed
 ½ **cup seasoned bread**
     crumbs
 ½ **cup Parmesan cheese**
  1 **whole egg**
  6 **drops of Tabasco sauce**
  2 **tsps. lemon juice**
  1 **Tbsp. mayonnaise**

Roast Duck with Pear and Avocado Sauce

Serves 8
Preparation Time:
  2 Hours
Preheat oven to 450°

  4 **ducks, approximately**
     5 lbs. each
     Fresh lemon juice
     Kosher salt
  1 **tsp. shallots**
  1 **tsp. clarified butter or**
     margarine
  2 **oz. Triple Sec**
     Juice of 1 fresh lime
 12 **slices of pear**
  2 **Tbsps. honey**
  1 **cup demi-glace**
 ½ **cup heavy cream**
  8 **slices of avocado**

To prepare the duck, poke 4 holes under the ducks' legs to help defat them while cooking. Coat thoroughly with fresh lemon juice and then sprinkle kosher salt over entire duck. Place ducks, breast side up, on roasting racks. Cook for 40 minutes or until lightly browned.

Reduce heat to 300° and turn ducks over. Drain the fat out of the pan. Cook 20 minutes and drain fat again. Turn ducks over one final time and cook 20 minutes more. Remove from oven and let cool. Once ducks are cool enough to handle, split them in half and remove back bone and breast bone from each half.

Just before assembling with sauce for serving, place duck halves on a cookie sheet, skin side up, with a little water in the pan to keep ducks from sticking. Place pan on bottom rack of oven with the broiler on high and cook until skin is crispy—approximately 5 to 7 minutes.

For the pear and avocado sauce, sauté the shallots in butter. Add Triple Sec and reduce. Add the remaining ingredients one at a time and continue to cook to desired consistency. Remove from heat.

To serve, place sauce directly on serving plate. Place ducks from broiler on top of sauce. Garnish top of ducks with alternate slices of pear and avocado in a fan shaped design.

Coconut Rum Caramel Custard with Roasted Banana Sauce

Stir 2 cups of granulated sugar, ¾ cup water and cream of tartar over low heat until sugar is dissolved. Let cook until the mixture turns light brown in color. Pour the caramel mixture into a two quart soufflé dish or into individual cups and swirl around to coat the sides.

Mix the whole eggs, egg yolks, and 1 cup sugar together gently in a bowl so that no bubbles form.

Bring 4 cups cream and the toasted coconut to a boil, remove from heat and slowly add to the egg mixture. Add the rum to the cream and egg mixture and pour through a fine sieve into molds.

Place the custard into a bain-marie and bake approximately 1½ hours or until done.

Roast the bananas at 450° until skin becomes dark brown and begins to ooze. Cool, peel and set aside.

Combine 1 cup sugar and ¾ cup water and caramelize over low heat. Add 1½ cup cream to the caramel and stir to cool down. Add the bananas and mix thoroughly. Strain through a fine sieve.

To serve, run a knife around the edge of the mold, invert the mold on a serving dish, and drizzle with custard banana sauce.

Trade Secret: Garnish with toasted coconut and several slices of banana for a truly decadent appearance.

Serves 8
Preparation Time:
  One Hour
Pre-heat oven to 350°

  4 cups sugar
1½ cups water
  ½ tsp. cream of tartar
  4 whole eggs
  8 egg yolks
5½ cups cream
  ¼ lb. toasted coconut
  ½ cup rum
  3 large bananas

❖

THE COONAMESSETT INN

REGIONAL AMERICAN CUISINE
Jones & Gifford Street
Falmouth
548-2300
Lunch daily 11:30AM–2:30PM
Dinner nightly 5PM–9PM
Sunday brunch Noon–3PM
AVERAGE DINNER FOR TWO: $50

The Coonamessett Inn beckons you for fine dining in a setting of magnificent gardens overlooking rolling hills and a tranquil pond. American regional cuisine is served elegantly in the Cahoon, Vineyard or Garden dining rooms. A casual lunch or dinner can be found in Eli's Lounge.

This classic New England hostelry focuses on fresh fish and seafood, such as its award-winning specialty of fresh lobster bisque, Coonamessett's Quahog Chowder and lobster pie.

Entrée choices may include a shrimp scampi sautéed with garlic, tomatoes, olive oil and Peccorino cheese, served over angel hair pasta or sautéed lobster meat with a cognac truffle cream.

CHEF DAVID KELLEY'S MENU FOR EIGHT

Lobster Cakes with Tomato Coulis

Sautéed Salmon in a Chardonnay Mussel Cream

Lobster Cakes with Tomato Coulis

For the lobster cakes, combine heavy cream and cubed bread in a bowl. Mix until cream is absorbed. Set aside.

In a large mixing bowl, combine the remaining ingredients, except the lobster meat, and mix until everything is incorporated.

Add the bread mixture to the wet mixture and blend together. Fold in the lobster meat and check seasoning. If mixture seems too loose, add dry bread crumbs.

Form lobster mixture into desired size cakes and lightly dust in flour. Sauté over medium-high heat in olive oil and cook each side for 2 minutes.

Serve warm with the tomato coulis. Recipe follows.

Serves 8
Preparation Time:
  25 Minutes

 1 lb. lobster meat, diced
 1 cup heavy cream
 6 cups fresh bread, cubed
 2 eggs, beaten
 2 Tbsps. Dijon mustard
 3 Tbsps. fresh herbs,
   chopped (basil, chervil,
   chives)
 1 tsp. dry mustard
 ½ green pepper, diced
 ½ red pepper, diced
 1 whole shallot, diced
 1 scallion, diced
   Juice of one lemon
   Tabasco, salt and pepper
   to taste
   Olive oil

Tomato Coulis

Yields: 2 Cups
Preparation Time:
  25 Minutes
Pre-heat oven to 450°

2 large shallots, peeled,
   thinly sliced
1 Tbsp. olive oil
2 lbs. tomatoes, peeled,
   seeded & chopped
2 cups dry white wine
   Salt and pepper to taste

I n a heavy saucepan, sauté the shallots briefly in olive oil until softened. Add chopped tomatoes and white wine and cook over medium heat until tender and most of the liquid has evaporated, about 15 to 20 minutes.

Transfer the tomato mixture to a blender and blend until very smooth. Season with salt and pepper.

Trade Secret: You may add fresh herbs to coulis for added color and flavor.

Salmon in a Chardonnay Mussel Cream

Prepare the sauce first. Soak the mussels in enough cold water to cover them. Add a dusting of dry mustard to the water to purge the mussels (this removes sand and grit). Soak for 20 minutes. Remove from water and debeard the mussels.

In a heavy gauge stockpot, heat 2 Tbsps. olive oil to the smoking point. Add the mussels, onion, carrot, celery, leek, garlic, thyme and pepper. Sauté, stirring constantly for 2 minutes. Add the wine, cover and simmer until the mussels are opened, about 2 minutes.

Remove the saucepan from heat and transfer the mussels to a bowl to cool. Remove the mussels from their shells and reserve.

Return the vegetables and wine to heat and add the stock. Add the cream and simmer for 5 minutes.

Strain through a fine mesh strainer, then add the mussels, butter, chives, and salt and pepper to taste. Set aside.

Season the salmon steaks with salt and white pepper. Dust in flour and sauté in 2 Tbsps. olive oil over high heat for 2 minutes. Place the skillet in a hot oven for 4 minutes. Turn salmon over and return to oven for 4 minutes. Remove from skillet and place on platter. Drizzle with sauce and serve immediately.

Trade Secret: You may want to thicken your sauce with a roux—a mixture of melted butter and flour cooked over low heat for 2 minutes.

Serves 8
Preparation Time:
  45 Minutes

  8 salmon steaks
  2 lbs. mussels
    Dry mustard
  ¼ cup olive oil
  ½ medium onion, diced
  1 carrot, diced
  1 celery stalk, diced
  1 leek, green included, diced
  3 garlic cloves, diced
  2 sprigs fresh thyme
  ½ Tbsp. cracked white peppercorns
  2 cups dry white wine
  2 cups fish stock
  2 cups heavy cream
  2 Tbsps. unsalted butter
    Snipped chives as garnish
    Salt and pepper to taste

Dan'l Webster Inn

CONTEMPORARY AMERICAN CUISINE
149 Main Street
Sandwich
888-3623
Lunch 11:45PM–4:00PM
Dinner 4:30PM–6:00PM
AVERAGE DINNER FOR TWO: $35

The gracious hospitality and heritage of this proud inn is conveyed in the Colonial New England decor and costumed servers. The original tavern built in 1692 was destroyed by fire in 1971 and rebuilt in a fashion that would satisfy modern tastes, yet generate the charm and warmth of the original structure.

The expansion included a gracious sunlit conservatory and a wine cellar equal to the finest in New England. The menu developed into contemporary American cuisine that has been awarded national recognition each year.

Regional dishes such as fresh swordfish topped with a sun-dried tomato butter and native Cape scallops sautéed with hand-filled cheese tortellini, then finished with fresh pesto share the menu with homemade soups, fresh salads, sandwiches and whole grain pizza.

CHEF ROBERT V. CATANIA'S MENU FOR FOUR

Grilled Duckling Salad

Macadamia and Cashew Crusted Striped Bass

Pineapple Marscarpone Velvet

Grilled Duckling Salad

Brush olive oil onto the duck breasts and season with salt and pepper. Grill until medium rare in center, about 8 minutes. Cool, then slice the breast thin at a 45° angle.

Place lettuce on 4 individual plates. Arrange duck slices on bed of lettuce and top with your favorite vinaigrette. Sprinkle tops of salads with chopped pecans.

Trade Secret: A garnish of edible flowers is a beautiful accompaniment to this salad.

Serves 4
Preparation Time:
 30 Minutes

2 duck breasts, ½ lb. each
2 Tbsps. olive oil
  Salt and pepper to taste
1 head Bibb lettuce
¼ cup pecan pieces

Macadamia and Cashew Crusted Striped Bass

Serves 4
Preparation Time:
 One Hour

⅓ cup unsalted
  macadamia nuts
⅓ cup unsalted cashews
¾ cup fresh unseasoned
  bread crumbs
¾ tsp. salt
  Pinch of cayenne pepper
4 striped bass filets,
  6 oz. each
½ cup flour
3 eggs, beaten
8 Tbsps. (1 stick) unsalted
  butter
2 Tbsps. vegetable oil
2 ripe mangoes
⅓ cup Riesling wine
1 Tbsp. fresh lemon juice
½ tsp. garlic, chopped
2 Tbsps. honey

In a food processor, finely chop nuts, bread crumbs, salt and pepper. Dredge boneless, skinless filets in flour. Shake off excess flour, then dip into egg wash and bread crumb mixture.

In a large sauté pan, sauté filets in 2 Tbsps. butter and vegetable oil. Cook until brown on each side.

Purée mangoes and set aside. In a small sauce pan, reduce wine with lemon juice and garlic until almost fully reduced. Add mango purée and honey. Season to taste with salt and pepper. Remove from heat and whip in butter.

Serve filets drizzled with the warm mango sauce.

❖

Pineapple Mascarpone Velvet

In a medium-sized sauce pan, melt the butter with lemon juice and brown sugar. Add split vanilla bean and ginger. Cook for 3 minutes while stirring over medium heat. Add the pineapple chunks and rum. Cook over medium-high heat while stirring for 8 minutes or until pineapple begins to soften.

Remove pineapple with slotted spoon and reserve, leaving liquid in pan over medium-high heat. Allow to reduce until a syrup texture is achieved.

Cool both pineapple and syrup, then combine and reserve.

Place mascarpone, cream, honey and lemon juice in an electric mixture and whip until a fluffy yet firm texture is achieved. Do not over-whip or it will separate.

In 8 tulip glasses, place 2 Tbsps. of pineapple mixture on the bottom. Top with 2 inches of mascarpone mixture, then top again with 2 tablespoons of pineapple mixture.

Garnish with a dollop of whipped cream and a mint leaf.

Serves 8
Preparation Time:
  3 Hours

  1 Tbsp. unsalted butter
  1 tsp. fresh lemon juice
  ¾ cup packed light
     brown sugar
  1 whole vanilla bean,
     split
1½ Tbsps. fresh ginger
     root, chopped
  ½ pineapple, cut into
     chunks
  ¼ cup dark rum
  1 cup mascarpone
     cheese
  1 cup heavy cream
  2 Tbsps. honey
  1 tsp. fresh lemon juice
     Whipped cream
     garnish
     Mint leaves, garnish

THE FLUME RESTAURANT

NEW ENGLAND CUISINE
Lake Avenue
Mashpee
477-1456
Dinner Wednesday–Saturday, 5PM–9PM,
Sunday, Noon–8PM
Lunch Saturday, Noon–2:30PM
AVERAGE DINNER FOR TWO: $25

Native foods are featured at The Flume. Native American, that is. The restaurant is owned and operated by a family of Mashpee Indians and the restaurant itself is set overlooking the mill pond. The casual atmosphere invites you to sit and relax next to the hearth and appreciate the rustic surroundings. Many Native American artifacts decorate the restaurant and a full bar where conversation is welcome, is located below the dining area.

Owner Earl Mills and his chef, Donald Peters, are Wampanoag Indians, and Mills is also Chief Flying Eagle, the chief of the Mashpee Wampanoags. Together they serve up dishes indigenous to the area.

Seafood is delivered fresh daily to the restaurant, as is a vast assortment of vegetables. Entrées are served with Portuguese bread and a choice of potato or vegetables, cole slaw or salad. The menu offers a variety of dishes. The fish is often prepared in several different ways, such as the fresh swordfish available broiled with anchovy butter, creole en casserole or as fish and chips. Broiled scrod may be served with lemon butter or lobster sauce. Other highlights include roast duckling with apple stuffing and natural gravy, and pot roast with pan gravy.

Appetizers are plentiful and range from fried clams to a simple cheese with crackers. The desserts are made fresh daily including homemade pies and puddings.

CHEF EARL MILLS SR.'S MENU FOR SIX

Escalloped Oysters

Fresh Poached Atlantic Salmon with Egg Sauce

Apple Brown Betty

Escalloped Oysters

Mix together the bread and cracker crumbs. Stir in the butter until mixture is well coated. Spread a thin layer, using half the crumbs, in the bottom of a shallow baking dish. Add the oysters and some of the oyster liquid and a pinch of salt. If light cream and Tabasco are used, add them together and "dribble" over the oysters.

Cover with the remaining crumbs and bake for 20 minutes or until edges are bubbling and crumbs are nicely browned. Garnish with parsley and lemon wedges.

Serves 6
Preparation Time:
  35 Minutes
Pre-heat oven to 400°

¼ cup coarse bread
    crumbs
½ cup coarse cracker
    crumbs (saltines)
¼ cup melted butter
 1 cup oysters with their
    liquor (18–22 oysters)
    Pinch of salt
    Dash of Tabasco,
    optional
 1 Tbsp. light cream,
    optional
    Parsley, garnish
    Lemon wedges, garnish

❖

Fresh Poached Atlantic Salmon with Egg Sauce

Serves 6
Preparation Time:
  45 Minutes

  6 **salmon filets, 8 oz. each**
  2 **Tbsps. butter or**
     margarine
  2 **Tbsps. flour**
  1 **cup warm milk**
     Salt and pepper to taste
  2 **hard-boiled eggs,**
     coarsely cut
  4 **cups water**
  3 **bay leaves**
  1 **Tbsp. vinegar**
  ½ **cup dry white wine**
     Parsley, chopped
     Lemon wedges

Clean the salmon filets and set aside.
Melt the butter over low heat and add the flour, stirring until blended. Cook until the mixture begins to look like corn meal, then add warm milk slowly, stirring constantly. Cook until the sauce is thick and smooth. Add salt, pepper and eggs. Set the egg sauce aside in a double boiler over low heat until you're ready to use.

In a fish poacher or large stock pot, combine the water, bay leaves, vinegar and a pinch of salt over medium heat. Add the wine and salmon filets and continue simmering until the fish is firm to the touch, about 10 minutes for each inch of thickness measured at the thickest part of the fish. Do not overcook!

Remove the filets, let drain and place on individual plates. Drizzle sauce over the filets and garnish with chopped parsley and lemon wedges.

Apple Brown Betty

Peel, core and slice apples and place in a small sauce pan. Add the water and granulated sugar. Cover and simmer over low heat until the apples become soft.

Grease a 4" × 8" loaf pan with 1 Tbsp. of butter and ½ tsp. of cinnamon. Mix the bread cubes and remaining butter lightly with a fork and add ¼ of the buttered bread to the bottom of the pan. Add half of the apples and top with another ¼ of the bread crumbs. Crumble half the brown sugar and half of the remaining cinnamon on top.

Repeat with layers of apples, bread, brown sugar and cinnamon. Cover with foil and bake for 25 minutes. Uncover and bake for 5 minutes more to brown and crisp.

Serve with ice cream or whipped cream.

Serves 6
Preparation Time:
  45 Minutes
Preheat oven to 350°

- 3 lbs. cooking apples, about 4 to 5 cups, diced
- ¼ cup water
- 1 tsp. granulated sugar
- 5 Tbsps. melted butter or margarine
- 2 tsps. cinnamon
- 6 slices fresh white bread with crust, cut into ½" cubes
- ¼ cup light brown sugar, firmly packed
  Ice cream or whipped cream

❖

HARBOR POINT RESTAURANT

SEAFOOD
P.O. Box 303
Cummaquid
362-2231
Lunch and Dinner 11:30AM–10PM
AVERAGE DINNER FOR TWO: $25–$30

Rumored to have been "a house of ill repute" and a site where bootlegging took place in the early 1900's, the Harbor Point Restaurant today is a charming establishment with a breathtaking view of Barnstable Harbor. The house was first built as a home for the Johnson family on 150 acres of salt marsh. Each of the four dining rooms has ocean views and offers elegant dining while the outdoor deck, adjoining a fully-stocked bar, gives guests a chance to enjoy the ocean air and an outdoor view of spectacular sunsets.

The menu pleases landlubbers and seafarers alike. Baked stuffed haddock, grilled swordfish and a lobster bake are three quintessential Cape Cod entrées, as well as prime rib of beef and Cornish game hen.

CHEF KEVIN ANDRADE'S MENU FOR TWO

Devils on Horseback

Asparagus & Artichoke Salad in Orange Raspberry Vinaigrette

Yellowfin Tuna Cape Codder

Devils on Horseback

Cut the bacon strips in half. Take half a strip and wrap it around the oyster using a toothpick to hold the bacon in place. Bake in Casino butter.

Sauté the leeks in casino butter and add brandy and reduce. Served over braised leeks.

Serves 2
Preparation Time:
   10 Minutes

12 plump oysters
 6 strips bacon
 2 bunches of leeks
    Casino butter (red &
    green peppers, garlic,
    lemon & butter)
 2 oz. brandy

Asparagus & Artichoke Salad with Orange Raspberry Vinaigrette

Serves 2
Preparation Time:
  10 Minutes

2 jars marinated artichoke
  hearts
2 cans white asparagus
  spears, drained
  1½ Tbsps. red onions,
  minced
1 Tbsp. yellow pepper,
  chopped
  Red leaf lettuce, cleaned
3 Tbsps. fresh orange juice
1 Tbsp. raspberry vinegar
¼ cup light olive oil
  Salt and freshly ground
  pepper to taste
2 tsps. snipped fresh
  chives

C ombine asparagus, yellow peppers, red onions, and artichoke hearts. Put all ingredients in artichoke marinade. Cover and let stand 2–4 hours at room temperature.

Place a bed of red leaf lettuce around the salad plate. In the center of the plate, place about 9 or more asparagus spears. Cut the artichoke hearts in half—two on each side—topped with red onions and yellow peppers.

Mix the orange juice and vinegar together in a small bowl. Slowly add the oil, whisking constantly until smooth. Season with salt and pepper, and stir in the chives. Makes ½ cup.

Pour dressing over salad and serve.

❖

Yellowfin Tuna Cape Codder

C oat the steaks with a little oil. Grill over a high heat.

Sauté the garlic, mushrooms and scallions for about 1 minute.

Dip the scallops and shrimp in flour. Sauté for about 2 more minutes. Add the butter and Marsala wine and reduce to desired consistency.

To serve, pour sauce over fish and top with scallops and shrimp.

Serves 2
Preparation Time:
10 Minutes

2 yellowfin tuna steaks, 10 oz. each
   Olive oil
2 garlic cloves, chopped
½ cup mushrooms, sliced
4 scallions, chopped
3 oz. bay scallops
2 jumbo shrimp
¼ cup flour
4 Tbsps. sweet butter
1 cup Marsala wine

❖

Napi's Restaurant

CONTINENTAL CUISINE
7 Freeman Street
Provincetown
487-1145
Dinner 5PM–10PM
AVERAGE DINNER FOR TWO: $30

Located on a winding street full of colorful sunflowers and roses—a block away from the hustle and bustle of the town—is a unique restaurant called Napi's. Here you will dine surrounded by works of local artists, antique stained glass, hanging plants and carousel horses.

Napi's is an institution in Provincetown, offering Portuguese, Middle Eastern, Moroccan, Oriental and European dishes.

The food at Napi's reflects the imagination and dedication to healthy lifestyles that the Van Derecks embrace. The leather-bound menu looks more like an novel than a menu and offers chicken, fresh seafood, beef, pasta, stir fry and a large selection of vegetarian dishes.

CHEF HELEN VAN DERECK'S MENU FOR FOUR

Empress Caps

Vegetable Curry

Carrot Cake

Empress Caps

Clean mushrooms, remove stems and dice enough mushrooms to fill 1½ cups. Set the remaining whole mushrooms aside.

In a saucepan, melt the butter and sauté the diced mushrooms with the onions until soft. Add the parsley, remove from heat and cool.

Add the grated cheeses to the mushroom mixture and just enough dry bread crumbs to bind.

Hollow out the whole mushrooms, then fill with the stuffing mixture and place under a broiler until thoroughly heated and browned on top, about 5 minutes.

Serve immediately.

Serves 4
Preparation Time:
  30 Minutes

1½ **pounds large**
      mushrooms
  8 **Tbsps. (1 stick) butter**
  1 **cup onions, finely**
      diced
  ¼ **bunch parsley, finely**
      chopped
  ⅛ **cup Swiss cheese,**
      grated
  ⅛ **cup mozzarella cheese,**
      grated
  ⅛ **cup Parmesan cheese,**
      grated
      Dried bread crumbs

❖

Vegetable Curry

Serves 4
Preparation Time:
30 Minutes

One block tofu cut into
½" cubes
⅛ cup canola oil
Tamari sauce
Sesame oil
½ cup onions, sliced
½ cup mushrooms
½ cup red peppers, diced
½ cup broccoli, chopped
½ cup cauliflower florets
2 tsps. curry powder
Pinch of salt and black
pepper
½ cup soy milk or cream
1 tsp. tahini
¼ lb. fresh spinach leaves,
chopped
¼ cup green grapes, sliced
in half
1 banana, sliced
2 scallions, sliced
¼ cup toasted almonds

O ver medium-low heat, sauté the tofu in canola oil. Sprinkle with tamari sauce and sesame oil to taste and sauté for about 4 minutes to let the tofu absorb the flavors.

Add the onions, mushrooms, red peppers, broccoli and cauliflower. Lightly sprinkle with curry powder and add salt and pepper. Add the soy milk and reduce. The flavors will strengthen. Add the tahini.

Fold the spinach leaves into the tofu and vegetables and serve immediately. The spinach will cook from the heat of the vegetables.

Garnish with sliced green grapes, sliced bananas, sliced scallions and toasted almonds.

Trade Secret: Vegetable Curry is excellent over brown rice.

❖

Carrot Cake

I n a large mixing bowl, combine the wheat flour, brown sugar, baking soda, cinnamon, nutmeg, cloves and vanilla. Slowly add the oil and beaten eggs.

Stir in the carrots, raisins, walnuts, banana and pineapple. Pour batter into a lightly greased and floured 13" × 9" cake pan. Bake for 40–45 minutes.

In a mixer, cream the softened cream cheese and butter. Slowly add confectioners sugar, beating until fully incorporated (there should be no lumps). Stir in the orange juice and orange zest.

Frost the cake when cooled.

Yields: One 13" × 9" cake
Serves 10
Preparation Time:
  One Hour
Pre-heat oven to 350°

    2 cups whole wheat
        flour
    2 cups brown sugar
 2½ tsps. baking soda
    1 tsp. ground cinnamon
  ½ tsp. nutmeg
  ¼ tsp. ground cloves
    1 tsp. vanilla
    1 cup oil
    4 eggs, beaten
 1½ cups carrots, grated
  ¼ cup raisins
  ¼ cup walnuts, chopped
    1 large ripe banana,
        mashed
  ½ cup pineapple, diced
    4 oz. cream cheese,
        softened
    3 Tbsps. unsalted butter,
        room temperature
 1½ cups confectioners
        sugar
        Juice of 1 orange
        Zest of 1 orange, grated

THE PADDOCK

CONTINENTAL CUISINE
20 Scudder Ave
(at the W. Main Street Rotary)
Hyannis
775-7677
Lunch 11:45 AM–2:30PM
Dinner 5PM–10PM, Cocktails served until 1 AM
AVERAGE DINNER FOR TWO: $40

The Paddock restaurant has not always enjoyed success. The owners, John and Maxine Zartarian, broke a 35-year old history of failure for the establishment when they purchased The Paddock in 1969. Since then, the restaurant has flourished and has been voted the Best-Run Eatery in Bristol County by Business Digest.

The main dining room has low beam and plaster ceilings and dark paneling with Victorian furniture, linen-covered tables and fresh cut flowers. Guests dine by candlelight in elegant and sophisticated surroundings.

A refined menu parallels the decor of the restaurant and offers a broad selection of seafood, meats and poultry. Entrées like Paupiettes of Sole Oscar, which is fresh sole, crab meat, and asparagus topped with Bernaise sauce, and a baked sole, which is a healthful dish made with thin filets, stacked on top of one another and gently baked with Bermuda onion, snow peas and lemon vinaigrette are highlights from the seafood list. From the meat and poultry section, a Veal a la Maison, and Tournedos of Beef Rostand made from fine tenderloin and garnished with artichokes and mushrooms are two tempting entrées. Appetizers and soups are plentiful with choices such as herring, escargot and chilled raspberry soup.

CHEF JOHN ANDERSON'S MENU FOR TWO

Cioppino

Swordfish au Poivre

Chicken Breast with Artichokes and Shrimp

Cioppino

I n a heavy stock pot, place the cod, garlic, shallots, thyme, bay leaves, mushrooms and white wine. Place the clams, mussels, scallops and oysters on top and cover.

Bring to a boil and then simmer for about six minutes. Add the asparagus and tomatoes and heat for a few minutes. Season with salt and pepper to taste.

Serves 2
Preparation Time:
  30 Minutes

  1 lb. cod
  2 tsps. garlic, chopped
  2 tsps. shallots, chopped
  1 tsp. thyme
  2 bay leaves
1½ cups mushrooms,
    sliced
1½ cups white wine
  4 littleneck clams
  8 mussels
  6 scallops
  4 large oysters
  6 asparagus spears, cut
    on the bias, blanched
  2 tomatoes, peeled, cut
    into sixths
    Salt and pepper to taste

❖

Swordfish Au Poivre

Serves 2
Preparation Time:
  10 Minutes

  2 swordfish steaks,
    1″ thick
  6 Tbsps. cracked
    peppercorns
    Vegetable oil
½ cup brandy
¾ cup heavy cream
½ cup beef or veal stock
    Salt and pepper to taste

over one side of steak with peppercorns. Grill or sear steaks in a sauté pan over high heat in vegetable oil. Cook for 3 to 4 minutes per side.

Remove steaks from sauté pan and deglaze with brandy. Add the cream and stock. Salt and pepper to taste.

❖

Chicken Breasts with Artichokes and Shrimp

Lightly dust chicken breasts with flour. Sauté in a small amount of oil over high heat until golden brown. Pour off the cooking oil and add butter, shallots, and shrimp.

Add the lemon juice, mushrooms, artichokes and white wine. Reduce by half and add the stock and cream. Simmer until sauce is desired consistency.

Trade Secret: This dish is excellent over a rice pilaf.

Serves 2
Preparation Time:
  30 Minutes

2 chicken breasts,
   cut in half
   Flour
2 Tbsps. vegetable oil
2 Tbsps. butter
2 Tbsps. shallots, chopped
6 large shrimp
   Juice of 1 lemon
6 mushrooms, sliced
4 artichoke hearts
   cut in half
½ cup white wine
½ cup beef or veal stock
½ cup heavy cream

POPPONESSET INN

NEW ENGLAND CUISINE
Shore Drive
New Seabury
477-1100
Lunch Noon–3PM
Dinner 5PM–10PM
AVERAGE DINNER FOR TWO: $40

estled in the center of New Seabury, the Popponesset Inn has served traditional New England cuisine for the last 50 years. The inn is in a unique location providing fireside and oceanside dining with an expansive view of Nantucket Sound and Martha's Vineyard. The restaurant also has a unique honorary host, Poppy the parrot, who greets guests in the restaurant lobby.

The menu is simple, offering both traditional Cape Cod fare and elegant entrées with seafood and regional dishes as main focuses. A regional favorite, Chicken Nantucket, is a breast of chicken sautéed with shrimp, wild mushrooms and Marsala sauce. Seafood entrées are plentiful with highlights like the Lazy Lobster Pie made with chunks of lobster and drawn butter covered with a crumb topping, and the Seafood Sampler en Papillote made of scrod, swordfish, shrimp and scallops baked with leeks, carrots and wine. Daily specials are also offered by Chef David Schneider.

The appetizer list is dominated by seafood selections like fresh oysters on the half shell, smoked Norwegian salmon and a batter-fried coconut shrimp with orange radish.

A list of seasonal salads is also included as well as soups including the New England stand-by, clam chowder.

The dessert list is long and tempting. An old-fashioned ice cream puff with hot fudge sauce and the Poppy ice cream pie are just two of the selections, so be sure to bring an appetite.

CHEF DAVID SCHNEIDER'S MENU FOR EIGHT

New England Clam Chowder

Linguine with Salmon and Scallops Carbonara

Chicken Nantucket

New England Clam Chowder

n a sauté pan, prepare the roux by melting the butter. Add the flour and cook, stirring constantly, for 5 minutes.

Strain the clams from the juice.

In a large soup pot, heat the juice over medium heat. When hot, add the roux to thicken.

In a separate pot, boil or steam the onions and celery until tender. Boil or steam the potatoes until cooked but still firm. Add the cooked onions, celery and potatoes to the thickened clam broth. Add the chopped clams, cream and seasonings. Cook an additional 5 minutes. Serve immediately.

Serves 8
Preparation Time:
  One Hour

  8 Tbsps. butter (1 stick)
  6 Tbsps. flour
 46 oz. chopped clams
     with juice (about 2
     cups juice)
  2 onions, diced small
  1 bunch celery, diced
     small
  8 potatoes, diced
 1½ cups light cream
     Salt and pepper to taste
     Worcestershire sauce
     to taste

❖

Linguine with Salmon & Scallops Carbonara

Serves 8
Preparation Time:
  20 Minutes

  1 Tbsp. olive oil
  2 lbs. fresh linguine
  2 lb. salmon, poached,
    flaked
  2 lb. scallops
  1 lb. bacon, diced, cooked
  ⅓ cup Parmesan cheese,
    grated

Bring a large pot of water to a boil. Add the olive oil and linguine. Cook at a rolling boil until just tender. Drain, rinse under cold water, drain again, and set aside.

In a sauce pan over low heat, reduce cream in half. Add the salmon, scallops and bacon. Bring to a boil and add the cheese.

To serve, pour the cream mixture over the pasta and toss well.

❖

Chicken Nantucket

 Melt the butter in a large skillet. Dredge chicken breasts in flour, season with salt and pepper and place in skillet.

Sauté until half-cooked then add the shrimp. Cook for 2 minutes, turn shrimp and cook an additional 2 minutes. Add mushrooms and cook for 1 minute. Deglaze pan with wine and reduce slightly.

To serve, arrange shrimp on top of chicken breast, garnish with pea pods and drizzle with wine sauce.

Serves 8
Preparation Time:
  30 Minutes

 4 Tbsps. butter
 8 chicken breasts,
    boneless, skinless
    Flour
    Salt and pepper to taste
24 medium shrimp, peeled,
    deveined, tails off
 2 cups wild mushrooms,
    sliced (oyster, crimini or
    shiitake)
 1 cup Marsala wine
 4 dozen pea pods,
    washed, stemmed,
    blanched

THE RED PHEASANT INN

AMERICAN CUISINE
Route 6A
Dennis
385-2133
Dinner 5PM–11PM
AVERAGE DINNER FOR TWO: $50

I t is appropriate that the Red Pheasant is located in a 100-year-old barn in Dennis Village. A beacon of tradition and comfort, the barn was the perfect place for the original owner, William Atwood, Sr., to open the restaurant which embraces classic cooking and comfortable surroundings.

Decorated in antiques and knickknacks, the restaurant exudes an aura of elegance while remaining as comfortable as home. During the winter, guests can enjoy the dining room bathed in the warm, glowing light of the fireplace, or in the perennial greenhouse, bright with greenery and accented with paintings of gardens on the walls.

William Atwood, Jr. now presides as owner and chef of the Red Pheasant while his wife, Denise, is co-manager and hostess. Chef Atwood uses fresh, local ingredients to create his time-honored dishes as well as finding new, exciting and artistic ways to make and display them. The menu suits everyone by offering a large and varied selection.

Entrée highlights include a grilled swordfish served with fresh grilled vegetables and a square of polenta, a roast boneless duckling, and white fish stew.

For after dinner, a fine selection of ports and cognacs are available as well as a myriad of homemade desserts.

CHEF WILLIAM ATWOOD, JR.'S MENU FOR EIGHT

Tuna with Honey Wasabi Vinaigrette

Braised Pheasant in Beaujolais

Linzer Torte

Tuna with Honey-Wasabi Vinaigrette

Trim all dark meat from inside part of tuna and discard.

Prepare the marinade by combining salt, sugar, pepper, thyme, allspice, fennel, cloves, bay leaf and all water. Place tuna in brine and marinate for 4 hours, turning frequently. Remove from marinade. Strain brine.

Heat a heavy cast-iron skillet over high heat. When hot, sear the tuna on all sides. Remove from heat and chill immediately.

Prepare the grill to either smoke or cook the tuna.

In a separate bowl, add 3 Tbsps. water to the Wasabi and let stand for 10 minutes.

In a separate bowl, combine the soy sauce, olive oil, sesame oil, honey and vinegar. Add the Wasabi paste and mix thoroughly.

Toss the vinaigrette with the lettuce mix so it is lightly coated.

To assemble, top lettuce mixture with tuna, garnish with capers and red onion.

Serves 8
Preparation Time:
 5 Hours
(note marinating time)

- ½ **cup salt**
- 1½ **Tbsps. sugar**
- 1 **Tbsp. cracked black pepper**
- 4 **tsps. fresh thyme**
- 1 **tsp. allspice**
- 1 **tsp. fennel seed**
- 2 **cloves**
- 1 **ground bay leaf**
- 4 **cups water**
- 5 **lbs. tuna, center cut loin**
- 6 **Tbsps. Wasabi, dry**
- ¼ **cup soy sauce**
- 1 **cup olive oil**
- ¼ **cup sesame oil**
- ½ **cup honey**
- 1½ **cups vinegar**
- 1 **lb. baby lettuce mix, cleaned**
  Capers, garnish
  Red onion slices, garnish

❖

Braised Pheasant in Beaujolais

Serves 8
Preparation Time:
  45 Minutes

  4 **pheasants, 3 lbs. each**
  ½ **cup peanut oil**
  1 **cup Beaujolais**
  ⅓ **lb. bacon**
  6 **Tbsps. butter**
  2 **cups cider or apple juice**
  3 **Golden Delicious apples,**
     peeled, sliced
  1 **head red cabbage,**
     shredded
  ½ **cup cider vinegar**
  3 **shallots, diced**
  1 **cup demiglace**

Split and bone pheasants, take off the breast plate and remove the thigh bone. Remove breast from thigh and leg. Tie the thigh with butcher's twine so it regains its correct shape.

In a large saucepan over medium heat, sear pheasant breast and legs on both sides in oil. Add the Beaujolais and deglaze, cover and simmer. The breast will cook before legs are done, so remove it and reserve in a warm spot. Turn heat on high and finish legs. Add breasts back into the glaze at the end. Reserve and keep warm.

While pheasants are simmering in Beaujolais, cook the bacon in another heavy saucepan. Add butter, cabbage, ½ cup cider and simmer for 5 minutes, covered. Add apples, turn heat to high and cook until liquid reduces and cabbage is tender, uncovered. Reserve and keep warm.

For the sauce, pour cider vinegar into brazier and deglaze Beaujolais juices and add shallots. Reduce to half. Add cider, reduce to half. Add demiglace and finish to desired consistency.

To assemble, sauce plates, put pheasant on top with the cabbage, apples and bacon around pheasant.

❖

Linzer Torte

 R oast hazelnuts in a hot oven until the skins blister. Remove skins and put nuts into a food processor. Pulse until nuts are ground roughly but not too fine.

In a mixer or food processor, cream the butter and sugar. Add the eggs one at a time. Add the vanilla.

In a large mixing bowl, combine the flour, nuts, cinnamon, and baking powder. Mix in the buttered sugar mixture.

Roll the pastry out on a lightly floured surface. Take ¾ of the dough and press into the bottom of the cake pan and half-way up the sides. Spread the raspberry preserves over the dough. Roll out remaining dough and cut into thin strips to make a lattice pattern on top. Bake for 45 minutes or until the crust is golden.

Makes one 10″ tart
Serves 8
Preparation Time:
  One Hour
Pre-heat oven to 350°

  ¾ **lb. hazelnuts**
 16 **Tbsps. (2 sticks) sweet**
    whole butter
 1½ **cups sugar**
  2 **large eggs**
  1 **tsp. vanilla**
  2 **cups flour**
  4 **Tbsps. cinnamon**
  2 **tsps. baking powder**
 1¼ **cups raspberry**
    preserves

❖

THE REGATTA OF COTUIT

AMERICAN CUISINE
Route 28
Cotuit
428-5715
Dinner 5:30PM–10PM
AVERAGE DINNER FOR TWO: $60

T he Regatta of Cotuit is located in the eighteenth-century Crocker House. It is rumored that guests can still hear laughter from times gone by as they cross the threshold of the 200-year-old federal mansion.

The guests of the Regatta dine by candlelight in any one of the eight intimate dining rooms. The restaurant is decorated with authentic wallpapers and Williamsburg colors and has one-of-a-kind Bernardaud Limoges. The tables are elegantly draped in delicate pink and sand-colored napery and set with fine crystal and silver settings.

The menu reflects the elegance of the surroundings and offers a variety of seafoods and meats in an ever-changing array of dishes. Chef Martin Murphy takes care that only the freshest and most exciting seasonal products make it to your table.

Seafood highlights include a Thai steamed Sole in Satay Sauce, grilled center cut of Swordfish with a Cilantro and Lime Vinaigrette, and native Lobster with a Saffron Fettuccine with Saffron Cream Sauce. Meat entrées include game, poultry and beef. A sautéed Quail with Wild Rice, and a seared loin of Venison served with Caramelized Pear and a Rosemary Wine Sauce are just two of the seasonal game items on their menu.

Soups and appetizers are plentiful and include items like the native Plum Tomato and Basil Soup, a Scallop Bisque, Country Paté, and Maryland Soft Shell Crab in a Three-Pepper Vinaigrette.

CHEF MARTIN MURPHY'S MENU FOR FOUR

Acorn Squash Bisque

Roasted Stuffed Quail, in Sauce Madeira

Hand-Dipped Chocolate Strawberries

Acorn Squash Bisque

Split and deseed the squash. Bake until soft, trying to keep the squash from discoloring. Remove the pulp and juice, discarding the skin. Set aside.

Dice the celery (with leaves), onion, and carrot. Sauté in butter until vegetables soften. Add the sliced apples, cook briefly and add the squash.

Add the Chardonnay and cook to reduce slightly, stirring constantly. Add stock and reduce. Season with spices, taste and add a pinch of brown sugar if needed. This depends on the squash.

Strain through a fine mesh, return to soup pot and finish with cream over low heat. Season with salt and pepper before serving.

Serves 4
Preparation Time:
  1½ Hours
Pre-heat oven to 325°

2 **large acorn squash**
2 **Tbsps. butter**
1 **stalk celery, with leaves**
1 **small red onion**
1 **carrot**
2 **green apples, sliced**
1 **cup Chardonnay**
2 **cups chicken stock**
  Pinch of nutmeg,
  cardamom, allspice and
  cinnamon
  Brown sugar to taste
1 **pt. heavy cream**
  Salt and white pepper

Roasted Stuffed Quail, Sauce Madeira

Serves 4
Preparation Time:
  45 Minutes
Pre-heat oven to 400°

4 quail, semi-boneless,
  unsplit
1 Tbsp. salt pork
2 Tbsps. smoked bacon,
  minced
3 lbs. mushrooms,
  stemmed
1 lb. shiitake mushrooms
3 shallots, peeled, finely
  minced
½ cup Madeira
1 cup veal or beef stock
2 Tbsps. demi-glaze

S auté the salt pork and bacon over low heat until crisp.

In a food processor with steel knife attachment, pulse mushroom caps until finely chopped. Repeat procedure with shiitakes.

Add both mushrooms and shallots to the pork and sauté until just moist, then add the Madeira and reduce by half.

Add the veal or beef stock and bring to a boil, stirring occasionally. Reduce heat to a simmer then add the demi-glaze and cook until almost all liquid has evaporated and the mushrooms have set. Remove from heat and cool.

With a small spoon place approximately 2 Tbsps. of the mushroom mixture in each quail cavity. Stuff until plump.

Place quail on buttered 5" × 5" tinfoil square, fold foil halfway up the quail and cook for 8 to 10 minutes or until golden brown.

Hand-Dipped Chocolate Strawberries

C arefully rinse strawberries and dry thoroughly. Melt dark chocolate in a double boiler over low heat just until the chocolate is of a syrup consistency. Do not overheat.

Dip and cover berries in chocolate and leave at room temperature for half an hour for chocolate covering to harden.

Melt white chocolate in the same way. Then dip dark chocolate-covered strawberries halfway in white chocolate and refrigerate.

Serve the strawberries the same day they were dipped so they remain fresh.

Serves 4
Preparation Time:
   15 Minutes
(note refrigeration time)

12 large ripe strawberries, with stems still on if possible

12 oz. semi-sweet dark chocolate

12 oz. semi-sweet white chocolate

❖

THE REGATTA OF FALMOUTH-BY-THE-SEA

CLASSIC FRENCH CUISINE
217 Clinton Avenue
(at the Falmouth Harbor entrance)
Falmouth
548-5400
Dinner 5:30PM–10PM
AVERAGE DINNER FOR TWO: $60

Considered by many the most beautiful and romantic restaurant on the waterfront, the Regatta of Falmouth-by-the-Sea offers highly acclaimed French and American cuisines as well as a stunning location. The 100 seat restaurant sits at the entrance of Falmouth Harbor and is decorated in soothing pinks and mauves. The restaurant has delicate pink and mauve napery and Limoges porcelain and hand-blown oil lamps on each table. It also commands a spectacular view of sailboats entering and leaving the biggest harbor in Cape Cod.

Chef Vincent Ditello creates dishes pleasing to the palette and to the eye. A Regatta signature entrée, the Rack of Lamb en Chemise, is a tempting entrée made of lamb surrounded by chèvre, spinach, and pine nuts, wrapped in puff pastry and served with cabernet sauvignon sauce. Sautéed Maryland Soft Shell Crab is made with an opal and green basil beurre blanc. The Thai Lobster and Shrimp with Ginger, Cilantro and Asian Greens is a New England favorite with an Eastern flair. Appetizers include a Paté of Smoked Bluefish with Horseradish Sauce, Chilled Oysters with a Three-Pepper Mignonette and Wild Mushroom Strudel.

CHEF VINCENT DITELLO'S MENU FOR FOUR

Vegetable Raviolis with Ginger Soy Dipping Sauce

New England Sea Scallop Bisque

Soft Shell Crab with Bacon and Red Pepper Vinaigrette

Chocolate Seduction Cake

Vegetable Ravioli

Sauté the scallions and onions over medium heat in 3 Tbsps. peanut oil. Add the red and green cabbage and slowly braise until tender. Add the vinegar, wine, soy sauce and sesame seeds. Simmer for 10 minutes. Remove from heat and place in the refrigerator to cool.

In a small bowl, make a paste with the cornstarch and water. Place each won ton skin on a work surface and top with 1 Tbsp. of the cabbage mix in the center of each won ton. With fingers or pastry brush, coat the outside edges of each won ton with the cornstarch mixture. Fold edges of skin from one corner to the opposite corner and press firmly. Makes three vegetable raviolis per person.

To serve, cook the raviolis for 1 minute in boiling water then sauté at high heat in 3 Tbsps. peanut oil until crisp. Top with ginger dipping sauce. Serve immediately and garnish with sliced scallion and chives.

Serves 4
Preparation Time:
  30 Minutes

  1 **bunch scallions, thinly sliced**
  1 **onion, thinly sliced**
  6 **Tbsps. peanut oil**
  3 **cups red cabbage, shredded**
  3 **cups green cabbage, shredded**
  4 **Tbsps. vinegar**
  4 **Tbsps. white wine**
  2 **Tbsps. soy sauce**
  2 **Tbsps. sesame seeds**
  2 **Tbsps. cornstarch**
  2 **Tbsps. water**
 12 **won ton skins**
     Ginger dipping sauce, recipe follows
     Scallions, sliced, garnish
     Chives, garnish

Ginger Dipping Sauce

1 tsp. ginger, diced
1 tsp. garlic, diced
¼ cup soy sauce
1 Tbsp. hoisin
1 Tbsp. oyster sauce
1 tsp. chili paste
¾ cup peanut oil
1 bunch cilantro, chopped

 In a mixing bowl, combine all the ingredients together. Keep at room temperature.

New England Sea Scallop Bisque

Melt butter in a saucepan. Add diced onion, celery and leek and cook until soft. Add scallops and simmer on low heat for five minutes. Add wine and simmer for five more minutes. Add half-and-half and season with salt and pepper to taste. Bring soup to a boil and then reduce to a simmer for 15 minutes.

Remove from the heat and purée soup in a blender. Serve hot, garnished with sprigs of parsley.

Serves 4
Preparation Time:
   30 Minutes

3 Tbsps. butter
1 medium onion, diced
3 stalks celery, diced
1 leek, diced
1 lb. scallops
1 cup white wine
1 qt. half-and-half
   Salt and pepper to taste
4 sprigs parsley

Maryland Soft Shell Crab with Bacon and Red Pepper Vinaigrette

Serves 4
Preparation Time:
  30 Minutes
Pre-heat oven to 450°

  2 Tbsps. bacon, diced,
    cooked
  1 Tbsp. garlic, diced
  1 Tbsp. shallot, diced
  2 Tbsps. lemon juice
  2 Tbsps. roasted red
    pepper purée
  5 Tbsps. olive oil
  1 tsp. mustard
  8 soft shell crabs
  1 cup milk
  1 cup flour
1½ cups snow peas,
    sautéed

ombine the bacon, garlic, shallot, lemon juice, red pepper purée, 3 Tbsps. olive oil, and mustard. Set the vinaigrette aside.

To prepare the crabs, clean by removing gills and cutting ¼" off the face, and remove tails.

Place crab in milk for 1 minute, and then in the flour. Coat evenly. Heat 2 Tbsps. olive oil until hot and carefully place crab, top side down, in pan. Place crabs in oven for 4 minutes and turn over for 2 additional minutes.

To serve, top crabs with vinaigrette and garnish with sautéed snow peas.

❖

Chocolate Seduction Cake

Melt the unsweetened chocolate and 8 Tbsps. butter in a double boiler over medium heat. Add the sugar and half-and-half and stir until the sugar is dissolved. Add the eggs and whisk into the chocolate, then add vanilla.

To prepare the crust, finely grind the Oreo cookies and mix with 4 Tbsps. melted butter. Press crust into a spring-form pan.

Pour the chocolate mix into the crust and bake for 45 minutes.

Serve cake when cool with fresh raspberries.

Makes one 12″ cake
Preparation Time:
  One Hour
Pre-heat Oven to 350°

2½ oz. unsweetened
    chocolate
12 Tbsps. (1½ sticks)
    butter
1¼ cups sugar
¼ cup half-and-half
2 eggs
1 tsp. vanilla extract
½ box Oreo cookies
4 Tbsps. melted butter
1 lb. raspberries, fresh or
    frozen

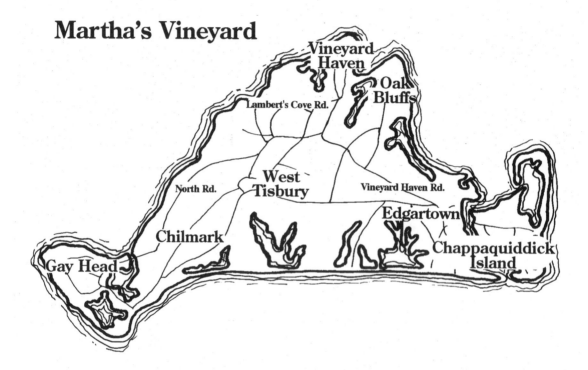

Five miles off the southern coast of Cape Cod lies a triangular island, Martha's Vineyard. About 20 miles long and nine miles at its widest point, Martha's Vineyard contains six towns: Vineyard Haven, Oak Bluffs, Edgartown (and the nearby island of Chappaquiddick), West and North Tisbury, Chilmark and Gay Head.

No one knows for sure for whom Martha's Vineyard was named. It is generally acknowledged that the first European to sight the island was English Captain Bartholomew Gosnold, who spotted it in 1602. But he did not bother to note his reason for naming it such. Historians conclude that he named it either for his daughter, Martha, or his mother-in-law, Martha Golding. The Vineyard part came from all the grapevines found on the island.

One other possible discoverer was Leif Ericson, the Norse adventurer. A boulder on a small nearby island, No Man's Land, bears the figure 1004 in eroded marks, prompting some authorities to conclude that the Norseman saw the island 600 years before Gosnold.

The place names found on Martha's Vineyard are a study in themselves. The resident Wampanoag Indians called the island "Noepe," or "Amid the waters." Edgartown originally was called "Nunnepog" or "Fresh Pond." But it was renamed in 1671 in honor of the infant son of the Duke of York. The Indians called Oak Bluffs "Ogkeshkuppe," or "Damp Thicket." West Tisbury originally was called "Tackhum-Min-Eyi" or "Takkemmy," "The Place Where One Goes to Grind Corn."

Vineyard Haven has had at least three names. Originally called Holmes Hole (any protected anchorage was called a "hole," just as "chop" is the old English word to describe the entrance to a harbor), the town changed its name to Vineyard Haven in 1872. And still later the town's name was legally changed to Tisbury. But Vineyard Haven is the more commonly used name, even though the visitor will note that Tisbury pops up sometimes.

No one seems to know the origins of the name of No Man's Land, a tiny island eight miles offshore. But it has always been isolated. While used as a fishing grounds and for raising sheep at one time, it is now owned by the U.S. government and is used for bombing practice.

MARTHA'S VINEYARD: Up and down

One other name of note is Gay Head. Called "Aquinnah," or "Long End" or "Point" by the Indians, the present name derives from 17th century sailors, who could see the multi-colored cliffs from out at sea.

Another piece of information that will help the visitor is understanding the difference between Up-Island and Down-Island. A leftover from the language of sailors, up or down do not refer to north and south, but to the degrees of longitude from Greenwich, England. When a ship sails east, toward England, its longitude goes down, ending in zero at Greenwich. And when it travels west, its degrees of longitude go up. So, the Down-Island towns are on the eastern and northeastern ends of the island. These include Vineyard Haven, Oak Bluffs and Edgartown. The Up-Island towns include West Tisbury, Chilmark and Gay Head on the west.

As with the other islands in the region, the beauty of the beaches and the sea are the biggest drawing cards. But Martha's Vineyard (the locals call themselves Vineyarders), attracts thousands of visitors to its inns, hotels, cottages, shops and restaurants.

Originally a community of farmers and fisherman, Martha's Vineyard became an important whaling center before the decline of the whale population and the discovery of petroleum as a source of oil brought the whaling industry to a halt. Then along came tourism to boost the economy.

So let's take a look at the visitors' destinations.

We'll begin with Vineyard Haven, the island's main port of entry and the commercial hub. Because of its strategic location and protected harbor, Vineyard Haven has long been a shipping center. Often sought as a refuge in stormy weather, the waterfront housed an enormous variety of nautical support services.

During the Revolutionary War, Martha's Vineyard struggled to remain neutral. But in 1778, British Major General Grey sailed into the harbor with 83 vessels, seeking supplies. For four days, Grey's men ransacked the area. Here is how one contemporary described it: "They carried off and destroyed all the corn and roots two miles around Holmes Hole Harbor; dug up the ground everywhere to search for goods the people hid, even so curious where they in searching as to disturb the ashes of the

*Osborn's Wharf,
Edgartown, with
the whaleship
"Splendid," circa
1867.*

*Looking over Lake Anthony
(the Oakbluffs Harbor), circa 1875.
The Sea View Hotel is in the
background. This pastime was
commonly called "Looking
over Jordan."*

dead." Grey's forces destroyed many ships and scores of whaleboats. Plus, they carried off 388 stands of guns, 1,000 pounds sterling, 300 oxen and 10,000 sheep.

Vineyard Haven today has more permanent residents than the rest of the island. And because it is the principal port of entry from the mainland, it is a pretty busy place. But you may wonder about the quiet at night: the sale of liquor is not allowed. Sights in around Vineyard Haven include the beautiful Greek Revival houses along William Street, William Barry Owen Park with its bandstand; the Katherine Cornell Memorial Theatre, the Jirah Luce House Museum and the West Chop Lighthouse about two miles from town.

Oak Bluffs is a fascinating town that owes its rise to the Methodists. While the Puritans and Quakers controlled other areas, the Methodists began in 1827 to hold camp meetings in Oak Bluffs. By the 1870s, a large tent was erected in the center of the Camp Ground.

Very quickly, "wooden tents" replaced the canvas models and the building boom was on. This was not an austere religion like some of the others, and the architecture reflects that difference. With more and more people building homes, a style called "Carpenter Gothic" took hold, with its gables, turrets, spires, scrollwork, balconies, intricate shingles and a rainbow of colors.

Another delightful invention of the encampment was the annual Illumination Night at the end of the summer. During the camp meetings, each tent was required to keep a lantern lit at night. But when developers came to the area, they came up with the idea of great masses of lanterns at night. In time—some say it was the result of a Japanese gift shop that opened in the area—the Illumination Night became a breathtakingly beautiful annual event.

Today, Oak Bluffs has a lot of offer. Trinity Park is a must—but you must do it on foot. The Park contains the historic Tabernacle and Trinity Methodist Church, with its stained cathedral windows. But it's the little gingerbread houses that will dazzle you with their wild array of colors and architectural decoration.

A popular stop is at the Flying Horses, one of the oldest carousels in America. Carved in 1876 by C.W.F. Dare, the horses were brought to Oak Bluffs in 1884 and have been very popular ever since.

❖

*Will Mayhew's store
at Edgartown,
circa 1894.*

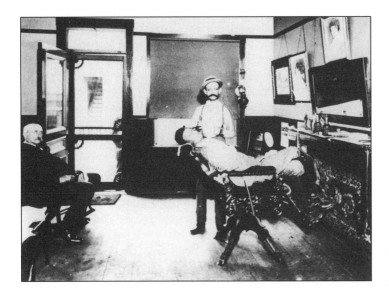

*A barber shop customer
covered with a fringed towel,
Edgartown, circa 1880.*

Ocean Park features a gazebo where band concerts are held in the evening.

Edgartown was the prosperous home port of the Arctic whaling fleet. In a typical year in the 19th century, the men kept busy by refining whale oil and making candles while the women turned out 15,000 pairs of socks, 3,000 pairs of mittens and 600 wigs. The resultant trade brought considerable wealth, so the town contains some fine homes built by successful merchants and seamen.

When whaling waned, so did Edgartown. But visitors from New York—including social arbiter Emily Post—discovered its charm and lovely homes. The refined new residents brought with them a more reserved outlook.

Edgartown's Cooke Street is the oldest street on the island. On its west end is the Edgartown Cemetery, with headstones dating from 1670, many inscribed with curious epitaphs. Also on Cooke Street are some of the oldest houses on Martha's Vineyard, including the Thomas Cooke House, circa 1766, now the headquarters of the Dukes County Historical Society. Here you will find the island's historical archives and an extensive collection of Colonial artifacts, plus over 100 logbooks from the whaling days.

Offshore from Edgartown is Chappaquiddick, made famous in recent years by Sen. Edward Kennedy. Chappaquiddick, which means "The Separated Island," may be reached by ferry from Edgartown. Among its attractions are the fine beaches on its eastern shores.

One historical footnote about Chappaquiddick involves Perry Davis, who was one of the owners of the island's corn gristmill. But his claim to fame was the invention of his Vegetable Pain Killer. A very popular patent medicine, its main ingredients were alcohol and opium. When it became a popular product, he moved his operation to another area.

Visiting the Up-Island communities of West Tisbury, Chilmark, Gay Head and North Tisbury will go much quicker than the populated areas.

West Tisbury, named for the English birthplace of former Gov. Thomas Mayhew, began as a light industrial area with a brickworks, lumber interests and a fish smokehouse. It features woodlands, open fields and equestrian trails. Music Street was so named, the story goes, because after one family bought a piano, every other family followed suit.

Chilmark is rural in nature, with windswept beaches, rolling hills, moors, and houses built at a distance. Its rural nature and cheap rents in the 1920s and '30s attracted a noted group of liberals and radicals. Frequent summer visitors included Norman Thomas, Felix Frankfurter and Walter Lippmann.

Gay Head, noted for its colorful cliffs, is an Indian township. Gay Head Indians were much sought after as whalers. Not only were they brave, but they were considered good luck. Tashtego, a character in Herman Melville's "Moby Dick," was from Gay Head.

North Tisbury has long been noted for its love of privacy. Along with West Tisbury, the area dominates a north-to-south-chunk of Martha's Vineyard. North Tisbury features rural charm and quiet, unhurried beauty. ❖

Vacationers in Cottage City, Oak Bluffs, circa 1880.

ANDREA'S RESTAURANT

ITALIAN CUISINE
137 Main Street
Edgartown
627-5850
Dinner 6PM–10PM
AVERAGE DINNER FOR TWO: $56

 ndrea's is a taste of northern Italy in downtown Edgartown. Created by Vera and Walter Dello Russo, the romantic restaurant is housed in a century-old whaling captain's house and features two small dining rooms with a wine-cellar lounge tucked in the basement.

On hot summer nights, the enclosed wrap-around porch of the restaurant is the perfect place for enjoying a meal, and a beautifully landscaped rose garden is open for al fresco dining in July and August as well. The intimate lounge offers live jazz Friday and Saturday nights as well as a place for late-night diners to enjoy an after-dinner cocktail.

The menu features traditional northern Italian favorites as well as lighter nouvelle cuisine and special additions are made by the chef daily. Entrées range from Pasta Puttanesca made with white or red garlic, olive oil, black olives, capers and finely chopped plum tomatoes to the spicy dish, Lobster Fra Diavolo, made with lobsters, scallops, clams and mussels smothering a plate of pasta. Hot and cold appetizers are offered such as Martha's Vineyard's own Littleneck Clams on the Half Shell, Pan-Fried Seafood Cakes and Prosciutto de Parma with Fresh Fruit. In addition to the printed menu, there are chef's additions every day. Desserts are mouth-watering and plentiful; cappuccino and espresso are served.

CHEF WALTER DELLO RUSSO'S MENU FOR FOUR

Clams Casino

Linguine Picante

Lobster Fra Diavolo

Clams Casino

Shuck clams and loosen meat from shells. Arrange in shallow baking dish over rock salt. If rock salt is not available, add ¼" water to the pan.

In a mixing bowl, blend the butter with garlic, white wine, salt, pepper, scallions and lemon juice. Spoon the butter mixture over each clam. Sprinkle red and green peppers over the butter. Place a piece of bacon or prosciutto on each clam. Drizzle Pernod over clams.

Bake for 20–30 minutes. Serve with lemon wedges.

Serves 4
Preparation Time:
  20 Minutes
Pre-heat oven to 425°

14 littleneck clams (about
   the size of a silver dollar)
   Rock salt or water if
   rock salt is not available
8 Tbsps. (1 stick) butter,
   room temperature
2 cloves garlic, finely
   chopped
½ cup white wine
   Salt and pepper
2 scallions, finely diced
1 Tbsp. lemon juice
1 red bell pepper, finely
   diced
1 green pepper, finely
   diced
2 strips bacon or
   Prosciutto, cut into 1"
   pieces
1 Tbsp. Pernod
   Lemon wedges for
   garnish

Linguine Picante

Serves 4
Preparation Time:
  15 Minutes

1 lb. linguine pasta
½ cup plus 1 Tbsp. olive oil
2 garlic cloves, chopped
½ tube anchovy paste or
  ½ can whole anchovies
1 cup black olives,
  chopped
1 cup green olives,
  chopped
1 Tbsp. capers
1 cup hot cherry peppers,
  chopped
½ cup scallions, chopped
½ cup Parmesan cheese
  Pinch of salt
1 tsp. crushed red pepper
. 1 cup bread crumbs
¼ cup parsley, chopped

I n boiling salted water, cook the pasta al dente, until firm yet tender. Remove from heat, drain and toss with 1 Tbsp. olive oil to prevent pasta from sticking. Set aside.

Sauté the garlic and anchovy in a saucepan over low heat until slightly browned in ½ cup olive oil. Add both black and green olives, capers, hot cherry peppers and scallions. Heat through.

Add the Parmesan cheese, salt and red pepper. Let simmer about 5 minutes.

Add the cooked pasta and toss together until the pasta is well coated with sauce. Top with bread crumbs and parsley.

Lobster Fra Diavolo

In a large deep sauté pan or stock pot, sauté the garlic in olive oil until the garlic starts to brown. Add the tomatoes with juice and bring to a boil. Reduce heat to simmer.

Add the fish stock, scallions, wine, oregano, thyme, nutmeg, bay leaf, Worcestershire sauce, Tabasco and red pepper. Simmer for 10 minutes.

Add the whole lobster, shrimp, scallops, clams and mussels. Cover and simmer until shellfish start to open. Remove cover and cook until shrimp and lobster are fully cooked.

Serve in soup bowls or over cooked pasta. Garnish with chopped parsley.

Serves 4
Preparation Time:
  30 Minutes

 2 **garlic cloves, chopped**
½ **cup olive oil**
   Two 28 oz. cans plum
   tomatoes with juice
 2 **cups fish stock**
 1 **scallion, chopped**
½ **cup red wine**
¼ **tsp. oregano**
¼ **tsp. thyme**
   Pinch of nutmeg
 1 **bay leaf**
½ **tsp. Worcestershire**
   sauce
½ **tsp. Tabasco**
½ **tsp. crushed red pepper**
   Two 1½ lb. lobsters cut
   in half lengthwise
12 **shrimp, peeled and**
   deveined
½ **lb. scallops**
12 **littleneck clams**
14 **mussels**
¼ **cup parsley, chopped,**
   for garnish

L'ÉTOILE

CONTEMPORARY FRENCH CUISINE
At the Charlotte Inn
South Summer Street
Edgartown
627-5187
Dinner 6:30PM–9:30PM
AVERAGE DINNER FOR TWO: Prix Fixe-$48 per person

Located on the first floor of the historic Charlotte Inn, L'Etoile is a contemporary French restaurant serving some of the best French cuisine on the island. The owners of the inn, Paula and Gery Conover have leased the restaurant for the last 2½ years to Chef Michael Brisson and his wife, Joan Parzanese.

The restaurant looks like an enclosed sunporch and the Conovers have decorated the 17-table dining room in crisp white linens, bright greenery and paintings of fruits and vegetables. The elegant restaurant is cozy and romantic at dinner, and bright and inviting at breakfast. The dining room also overlooks a 20-seat patio where guests can delight in an outdoor meal on a warm summer's night.

Chef Michael Brisson creates mouth-watering meals with fresh local fruits and greens, and the bounty of the Atlantic for his seafood. Menu highlights include native Lobster and Scallops with a Vegetable Taliatelle, and Roasted Lamb Noisettes with Warm Goat Cheese and Roasted Eggplant Millefeuille. Appetizers are just as inviting with items like Sautéed Ravioli of Rock Shrimp and Salmon Mousselines, and Ossetra Caviar with Mascarpone and Scallion-filled Crêpes. Fresh raspberries bought from local Thimble farm go into the White Chocolate and Raspberry Puff Pastry Tart, and L'Etoile's own Rhubarb Tart is a delicious creation.

CHEF MICHAEL BRISSON'S MENU FOR FOUR

Oyster and Spinach Custard with Saffron Beurre Blanc

Foie Gras with Mango and Raspberries

White Chocolate and Raspberry Puff Pastry Tart

Oyster and Spinach Custard with Saffron Beurre Blanc

Shuck the oysters, rinse and pat dry with towel. Steam the spinach and rinse it in cold water. Squeeze the liquid out and chop lightly.

Place the eggs and yolks in a blender and purée. Add 1¼ cups cream and spinach and pulse. Season with salt and white pepper. Combine 1 Tbsp. cornstarch and 1½ Tbsps. water, add to egg mixture and pulse.

Butter 4 molds (½ cup muffin tins or egg molds). Skim any foam off the top of the custard mixture. Fill the molds half way. Dredge the oysters in cornstarch shaking off any excess. Place two oysters in each mold. Fill the molds just shy of the top.

Place the mold in a bain-marie with water ¾ up the side of the mold. Cook for 18 minutes or until the custard is firm. Remove from oven and let cool 5 minutes. Prepare the beurre blanc sauce, by heating 3 Tbsps. white wine with the saffron. Reserve and set aside.

In a sauce pan, over low heat, reduce the vinegar, wine and shallots until there is barely any liquid left. Add 1 Tbsp. heavy cream, then whisk in the cold butter 1 Tbsp. at a time.

Remove from heat. Strain, season with salt and pepper and some of the saffron liquid to taste. Stir in the diced tomato just before serving.

With a small rubber spatula, free custards from the molds and drizzle with the sauce.

Serves 4
Preparation Time:
 35 Minutes
Pre-heat oven to 325°

 8 **fresh oysters**
1½ **cups spinach, cleaned**
 2 **extra large eggs**
 2 **egg yolks**
1¼ **cups + 1 Tbsp. heavy cream**
  Salt and pepper
 ½ **cup + 1 Tbsp. cornstarch**
1½ **Tbsps. water**
 ½ **cup + 3 Tbsps. white wine**
 6 **strands of saffron**
 3 **Tbsps. champagne vinegar**
 2 **Tbsps. shallots, chopped**
 8 **Tbsps. (1 stick) cold butter, sliced**
 2 **plum tomatoes, peeled, cored, diced**

❖

Foie Gras with Mango and Raspberries

Serves 4
Preparation Time:
  20 Minutes
(note refrigeration time)

  ¾ **lb. goose or duck liver**
  2 **Tbsps. cracked sea salt**
  2 **Tbsps. cracked white**
    pepper
  ½ **tsp. nutmeg**
  ½ **tsp. allspice**
1½ **Tbsps. shallots,**
    chopped
1¾ **cups leeks, julienne**
  3 **Tbsps. champagne**
    vinegar
  ⅓ **cup Muscat wine**
  ½ **cup chicken stock**
  1 **bay leaf**
  ⅓ **cup mango purée**
  1 **Tbsp. heavy cream**
  3 **Tbsps. cold butter**
    Flour
  ½ **pt. raspberries**
  2 **Tbsps. chopped chives**

Prepare the foie gras at room temperature. It is much easier to handle and will not tear when slicing. Separate the side lobe and remove the exposed veins and nerves by pulling gently with a towel. Lay the liver flat and cut it into ⅜″ slices. Season each slice with cracked sea salt, white pepper, nutmeg and allspice. Press the seasonings into the slices and chill.

For the sauce, sweat the shallots and ¼ cup leeks in the champagne vinegar until soft in a small saucepan. Add the Muscat wine and chicken stock, bay leaf and reduce by half. Strain, pressing the solids firmly against the strainer and discard.

Return the liquid to the saucepan and bring to a simmer. Whisk in the mango purée. Reduce to a ½ cup. Stir in the cream and simmer, then whisk in the butter and season with salt and pepper. Add 1½ cups leek julienne just to wilt it. Remove and reserve for garnish.

Heat a large sauté pan over medium-high heat. Coat the liver slices lightly with flour and place them into the pan. No fat is needed. Sauté each side 30 seconds for medium-rare. Place on a towel to drain any excess fat.

Arrange 5 raspberries in a star shape around the plate and wrap mango slices around the raspberries, looking like a flower. Ladle the sauce equally on the plates and place the foie gras in the middle of the plate. Arrange the wilted leek julienne over the top of the liver. Sprinkle with chives.

❖

White Chocolate and Raspberry Puff Pastry Tart

F or the tart shell, roll the puff pastry very thin to fit into the rectangular tart pan. Chill for 15 minutes and then with a fork, prick the dough so the rising is controlled.

Bake the tart shell until it starts to brown, about 18 minutes, then egg wash the shell and return to the oven for 5 minutes more until it is golden brown. Let cool for 10 minutes and then brush on the melted dark chocolate. This seals the tart shell from any moisture from the filling. Let cool at room temperature while making filling.

In a double boiler melt the white chocolate, butter, ¼ cup cream, and vanilla. Stir until mixture is melted and tepid.

Whip ¾ cup cream until soft peaks form and gently fold it into the white chocolate mixture until smooth. Do not over-fold. Pour filling into the pastry shell and dot with raspberries. Chill for 45 minutes.

Shave the white chocolate, at room temperature, with a vegetable peeler into a flat container to yield 3 cups. Chill 5 minutes in freezer.

When the filling has firmed, place the curls standing up on the tart. Cover the whole surface and chill until ready to serve.

Serves 4
Preparation Time:
   1½ Hours
Pre-heat oven to 350°

4″ × 12″ **tart pan with**
   removable bottom
1 **sheet of puff pastry, 6 oz.**
3 **oz. dark chocolate,**
   melted
1 **egg beaten with 1 Tbsp.**
   water for egg wash
6 **oz. white chocolate,**
   chopped
2 **Tbsps. butter**
1 **cup heavy cream**
2 **tsps. vanilla extract**
¾ **cup heavy cream**
   whipped to soft peaks
   White chocolate
   shavings, garnish,
   about 5 oz.

❖

LAMBERT'S COVE COUNTRY INN AND RESTAURANT

NEW ENGLAND CUISINE
Lambert's Cove Road
West Tisbury
693-2298
Dinner 6PM–9PM
Sunday brunch 11AM–1:30PM
AVERAGE DINNER FOR TWO: $56

T he Lambert's Cove Country Inn and Restaurant dates back to 1790. Located in a quiet and secluded setting, this elegant country inn is surrounded by 7 acres of lawns, gardens and vine-covered stone walls, apple orchards and towering pine trees.

The dining room setting is cozy and romantic, featuring hardwood floors, fireplace, soft lighting and music. The hearty New England cuisine features Island seafood, in-season vegetables just picked from nearby gardens, veal, beef, homemade soups, breads and delicious desserts.

Menu highlights include Duck Galantine with Pistachios and Olives, Grilled Swordfish Steak with a Brown Butter of Chunk Lobster, Macadamia Nuts and fresh Sorrel, and Roast Boneless Lamb Loin with a Mango Chutney.

The Sunday brunch menu features Strawberry Mascarpone filled Crêpes, Poached Salmon Filets with Hollandaise Sauce and Herb Roasted Potatoes or Cinnamon French Toast with warm Maple Syrup.

CHEF DAVID SCHMIDT'S MENU FOR FOUR

Shrimp, Scallops and Andouille Sausage Stew

Grilled Swordfish with Mangos and Sweet Peppers

Vanilla Mouse with Fresh Raspberries and Blackberries

Shrimp, Scallops and Andouille Sausage Stew

I n a 5-gallon stock pot, heat the olive oil and sauté the onions, celery, garlic and both bell peppers. When the celery and onions are translucent, add the Andouille sausage.

When the sausage is browned, add the quartered tomatoes and fresh basil. Let simmer for 5 minutes to start softening the tomatoes. Add the wine, saffron and spices and simmer for 15 minutes.

Add the rice, shrimp, scallops and 3 cups water. Make sure to add any juice from shrimp and scallops, since this adds a wonderful flavor. Simmer for 1 hour. Rice will absorb the excess liquid.

Trade Secret: This is excellent served with French bread or corn muffins.

Serves 4
Preparation Time:
  1½ Hours

3 Tbsps. olive oil
1 onion, minced
2 celery stalks, diced
2 cloves garlic
1 green bell pepper, diced
1 red bell pepper, diced
½ lb. Andouille sausage
6 tomatoes, quartered
3 Tbsps. fresh basil
2 cups white wine
6 threads saffron
½ tsp. ground coriander
½ tsp. ground cumin
1 cup rice
¼ lb. shrimp
¼ lb. scallops
3 cups water

Grilled Swordfish with Mangos and Sweet Pepper Relish

Serves 4
Preparation Time:
  30 Minutes

1 Tbsp. vegetable oil
2 tsps. fresh ginger, minced
1 tsp. fresh garlic, minced
2 Tbsps. Bermuda onion, minced
1 red bell pepper, diced
1 ripe mango, diced
  Pinch of curry powder
2 cups dry white wine
  Salt and pepper to taste
4 swordfish steaks, ½ lb. each, 1″ thick

In a small saucepan, heat the oil. Add the ginger, garlic and onion. Sauté until the onion is translucent. Add the bell pepper, mango, curry and white wine, and simmer for 10 minutes. Add salt and pepper to taste. Set aside.

Grill the swordfish steaks over high heat, about 3 to 4 minutes per side. The steaks should be seared on the outside and just cooked through, yet moist on the inside.

Serve immediately with the warm mango and sweet pepper relish.

❖

Vanilla Mousse with Fresh Raspberries and Blackberries

Combine the heavy cream, vanilla and ⅓ cup of the sugar in a mixing bowl. Whip until extra stiff. Do not over-whip or this mixture will not fold together with other ingredients. Place in a separate container and refrigerate.

In a small saucepan, combine ⅓ cup sugar with water over medium heat. Using a candy thermometer to determine when the syrup reaches 225°, begin whipping the egg whites together in a food processor or mixer at high speed. The egg whites will become stiff, with high points. (Do not turn off the mixer or the egg whites will fall.) When the syrup reaches 238°, turn the mixer to medium speed and slowly add the hot syrup. Mix the egg whites with syrup in mixer for 15 minutes on a low speed to cook the eggs.

After 15 minutes of mixing, fold the egg whites into the whipped cream. Fold both berries into the mousse mixture. Pour the mousse into individual ramekins and refrigerate for 1 hour.

Trade Secret: In this recipe, timing is very important. It is recommended that all measurements be made before starting the recipe. Fresh raspberry purée is a nice accompaniment to this dessert.

Serves 4
Preparation Time:
  45 Minutes
(note refrigeration time)

⅓ **cup heavy cream**
 1 **tsp. vanilla extract**
⅔ **cup sugar**
 2 **Tbsps. water**
 3 **egg whites, room**
   temperature
½ **pt. fresh raspberries**
½ **pt. fresh blackberries**

❖

THE OUTERMOST INN

AMERICAN CUISINE
RR 1, Box 171
Lighthouse Road
Gay Head
645-3511
Dinner seatings, 6PM and 8PM
AVERAGE DINNER FOR TWO: $70

T he Outermost Inn beckons visitors to enjoy an unbeatable location and the comforts of home. Hugh and Jeannie Taylor treat every guest like an old friend, making a stay at the Outermost almost too good to end.

The inn is in a perfect spot, set on the edge of rolling green hills with the stunning blue of the Atlantic just beyond. There are incredible views from all windows of the inn and guests can soak up the sun as well as the natural beauty of the surrounding areas. The inn is so friendly and relaxed that guests often return more than once.

Chef Barbara Fenner's cuisine is satisfying and artfully prepared. "People eat with their eyes and nose before they eat with their mouth," she says. Hence, the foods are aromatic and attractive. Even the butter on the tables is set in a unique arrangement—with oatmeal and onion-herb rolls on a clay flowerpot holder with a metal dish of butter at its center.

A favorite entrée of the chef is Striped Bass Stuffed with Oyster Dressing, baked and draped with Hollandaise sauce. All entrées are served with fresh cooked vegetables and crisp salads from local farms. Sesame Lemon Chicken in a lemon cream sauce and Shrimp Scampi are other entrées lovingly prepared.

Appetizers include Crab Cakes, Marinated Mushrooms, and a fresh fruit cup. Desserts are prepared fresh daily and include such items as an assortment of cheesecakes and a Blueberry Lemon Mousse.

CHEF BARBARA FENNER'S MENU FOR FOUR

Marinated Mussels

Seafood Stuffed Sole

Brownie Cheesecake

Marinated Mussels

Scrub the mussels in their shells under cold water and remove the beards.

In a Dutch oven, cook celery, onion, carrots, and garlic in the water and wine. Cover and simmer for 5 minutes.

Add the mussels to the mixture. Cover and simmer for 5 to 8 minutes, or until shells open.

Discard any unopened shells. Remove meats from shells. Slice the red peppers into strips ¼" wide by 2" long and set aside.

Combine oil, vinegar, mustard, Worcestershire sauce, salt and pepper, and blend together well.

Mix mussels and red peppers together with Dijon sauce and blend gently.

Serve at room temperature or chill for an hour.

Serves 6
Preparation Time:
30 Minutes
(note chilling time)

- 6 lbs. mussels
- ¼ cup celery, coarsely chopped
- ¼ cup onions, coarsely chopped
- ¼ cup carrots coarsely chopped
- ¼ cup garlic, coarsely chopped
- 4 cups water
- 2 cups white wine
- 6 large, sweet red peppers
- 3 Tbsps. virgin olive oil
- 1 Tbsp. red wine vinegar
- 1 Tbsp. Dijon style mustard
- 1 tsp. Worcestershire sauce
- ½ tsp. salt
- ¼ tsp. freshly ground black pepper

❖

Seafood Stuffed Sole

Serves 4
Preparation Time:
  One Hour
Pre-heat oven to 350°

  4 **sole fillets, 4 oz. each**
  1 **medium onion, diced**
  1 **cup celery, diced**
  4 **Tbsps. butter, melted**
  2 **cups white bread,**
    cubed
1½ **cups Ritz cracker**
    crumbs
  1 **lb. crab meat**
  1 **tsp. Worcestershire**
    sauce
    Mayonnaise
    Salt and pepper to taste

Sauté the onions and celery in 2 Tbsps. butter. In a mixing bowl, combine the cubed bread, cracker crumbs, and crab meat with the sautéed onion and celery. Add the Worcestershire sauce and blend in mayonnaise until the ingredients hold together well. Season with salt and pepper to taste.

Spoon ¼ cup of stuffing onto each fish filet. Roll the fish around the filling and arrange the fish rolls, seam side down, in a baking dish. Place any remaining stuffing around the fish rolls.

Brush butter over fish rolls and bake, uncovered, in a 350° oven for 20–25 minutes or until fish flakes easily.

Trade Secret: This dish is excellent topped with your favorite hollandaise sauce.

Brownie Cheesecake

F or the cake, melt the chocolate and 3 Tbsps. butter together in a double boiler.

Beat 2 eggs together, adding ¾ cup sugar in small amounts until mixed well. Let the chocolate mixture cool slightly and add it to the egg mixture. Stir well.

Combine the baking powder, salt, ½ cup flour, and nuts. Add this to the chocolate mixture. Stir in the almond extract and 1 tsp. vanilla.

For the topping, blend cream cheese and 2 Tbsps. butter until smooth. Add ¼ cup sugar, 1 egg, 1 Tbsp. flour, and ½ tsp. vanilla and mix well.

Pour two-thirds of the chocolate batter in an 8″ cheesecake pan, greased and lined with wax paper. Then spread the cream cheese mixture on top of the chocolate base. Spoon the remaining chocolate batter over the topping. Run a knife through the batter, marbleizing the two mixtures.

Bake for 35 minutes, or until a cake tester comes out clean.

Cool overnight in the refrigerator. Unmold when fully refrigerated.

Serves 8
Preparation Time:
   1½ Hours
Pre-heat oven to 350°
(note refrigeration time)

   4 oz. semi-sweet
      chocolate
   5 Tbsps. butter
   3 eggs
   1 cup sugar
   ½ tsp. baking powder
   ¼ tsp. salt
   ½ cup all-purpose flour
      (do not sift), plus
      1 Tbsp.
   ½ cup walnuts, coarsely
      chopped
   ¼ tsp. almond extract
   1½ tsp. vanilla extract
   3 oz. cream cheese

THE OYSTER BAR

AMERICAN CUISINE
162 Circuit Avenue
P.O. Box 1594
Oak Bluffs
693-3300
Dinner nightly 6PM–11PM
AVERAGE DINNER FOR TWO: $45

T he Oyster Bar was the restaurant that almost wasn't, but chef/owner Raymond Schilcher would not let a tight budget and very little time stop him. With the help of friends, the restaurant was created and has become a culinary asset to the Vineyard.

The restaurant blends such opposites as turn-of-the-century architecture with Rez William's paintings and pink neon to create its bistro-type appeal. The restaurant is open and exposed and yet every table offers some privacy. It is a place to relax and share a party environment with 100 people you don't even know. As Raymond Schilcher puts it, "It's food for thought and restaurant as theater."

Schilcher's style of cooking is straightforward and not gimmicky. This is people food; you don't have to be a critic to know you like it and that it tastes good!

CHEF RAYMOND SCHILCHER'S MENU FOR SIX

Oyster Fritters with Remoulade Sauce

Split Pea Soup with Dark Rum

Pasta with Cilantro Pesto

Rosemary & Garlic Oven-Roast Potatoes

Ratatouille

Tenderloin with Roquefort, Garlic Cream Sauce

Oyster Fritters with Remoulade Sauce

I n a large mixing bowl, make the batter by combining 1 cup flour, baking powder, ½ tsp. salt, eggs, beer or cream, butter, ½ tsp. Tabasco and nutmeg.

Dredge the oysters in 1 cup flour and then into the batter. Heat the oil to 375°F and fry the oysters until they are puffed and golden brown (about 4 minutes). Remove from oil and drain on paper towels.

Serve with lemon wedges and Remoulade sauce.

Serves 6
Preparation Time:
  30 Minutes

  2 cups flour
  1 tsp. baking powder
  ½ tsp. salt
  2 eggs
  ¾ cup beer or light cream
  1 tsp. melted butter
  ½ tsp. Tabasco
    Pinch of nutmeg
 18 shucked oysters
    Oil for deep frying
  1 lemon, cut into wedges
    Remoulade sauce,
    recipe follows

❖

Remoulade Sauce

Yields: 1½ Cups
Preparation Time:
  20 Minutes
(note refrigeration time)

2 egg yolks
1 tsp. salt
1 tsp. Tabasco
1 tsp. Dijon mustard
  Juice of 1 lemon
1 cup vegetable oil
1 Tbsp. cornichons,
  chopped
1 Tbsp. capers, chopped
1 Tbsp. parsley, chopped
1 Tbsp. dill, chopped
  Salt and pepper to taste

I n a large mixing bowl, combine the egg yolks, salt, Tabasco, mustard and lemon juice. Beat well.
Whisking vigorously, add the vegetable oil a little at a time in a steady stream until the sauce begins to thicken to desired consistency.
Add the cornichons, capers, parsley and dill. Adjust seasonings to taste. Refrigerate covered until ready to use.

Trade Secret: If remoulade is too thick, dilute with heavy cream and if it is too thin, add more oil.

Split Pea Soup with Dark Rum

Wash beans in cold water and sort out any impurities. Cover with boiling water and let sit 4 hours or overnight. Drain.

Over medium-low heat, sauté the bacon in oil until lightly browned. Remove bacon and reserve. Add the onions and carrots and cook, stirring, until soft. Add the garlic and cook 1 minute more. Add the reserved bacon and the remaining ingredients.

Simmer, covered, for 2 hours, stirring occasionally until peas are cooked through. If soup is too thick, add more water. Adjust seasonings to taste.

Trade Secret: The dark Alsatian beers are rich and would work as wonderful replacements to the dark rum.

Serves 10
Preparation Time:
　2½ Hours
(note soaking time)

 1　**lb. dried split peas**
 4　**oz. bacon, diced**
¼　**cup oil**
 2　**medium onions, diced**
 4　**carrots, diced**
 1　**Tbsp. garlic, minced**
 2　**cups whole peeled**
　　tomatoes, crushed
　　with juice
 3　**qts. stock: chicken,**
　　vegetable or ham
 1　**bay leaf**
½　**tsp. black peppercorns,**
　　crushed
 1　**lb. smoked ham, minced**
　　Juice of 1 lemon
¼　**cup dark rum**
　　Salt and pepper to taste

❖

Pasta with Cilantro Pesto

Serves 6
Preparation Time:
  20 Minutes

1 lb. linguine or fettuccine
  pasta
1 cup basil leaves,
  washed, dried
½ cup cilantro leaves,
  washed, dried
1 cup olive oil
6 cloves garlic, minced
1 tsp. salt
¼ cup pine nuts, almonds
  or walnuts
¼ cup Parmesan cheese,
  grated

C ook pasta in boiling salted water until al dente, firm yet tender.

In a food processor, purée the basil and cilantro, adding the oil in a slow, steady stream. Add the remaining ingredients and process until smooth. Adjust seasonings and add more oil or cilantro, depending upon finished consistency.

Drain pasta and toss with pesto. Garnish with additional Parmesan cheese if desired.

Trade Secret: This pesto freezes well or can be refrigerated for up to 2 weeks.

Rosemary and Garlic Oven-Roast Potatoes

T he potatoes should be no larger that 1″ diameter, all others should be cut in half.

Clean potatoes well and toss with the remaining ingredients.

Roast in oven, turning frequently, until golden and cooked through, about 30 minutes.

Trade Secret: These potatoes are a great accompaniment to roast leg of lamb. Any leftover potatoes can be cut into smaller pieces and sautéed for morning hash browns.

Serves 8
Preparation Time:
  40 Minutes
Pre-heat oven to 500°

3 lb. new red potatoes
½ cup olive oil
1 tsp. paprika
8 sprigs fresh rosemary
8 cloves garlic
  Salt and pepper to taste

❖

Ratatouille

Serves 6
Preparation Time:
 45 Minutes
Pre-heat oven to 450°

1 large eggplant, cut into
  spears
2 medium zucchini,
  cut into spears
1 medium leek, julienne
2 red bell peppers, cored,
  seeded, cut into spears
2 green bell peppers,
  cored, seeded, cut into
  spears
4 Tbsps. kosher salt
8 garlic cloves, peeled
3 large beefsteak
  tomatoes, seeded,
  cut into wedges
1 Tbsp. fresh thyme
1 Tbsp. fresh oregano
½ cup olive oil
  Salt and black pepper
  to taste

Toss the eggplant, zucchini, leeks and peppers with salt and let stand, covered, for 30 minutes to draw out excess water and reduce bitterness in the eggplant.

Rinse off salt and pat dry with towels. Toss with remaining ingredients and roast, uncovered, in the oven.

Turn vegetables every 5 minutes until done, about 25 minutes.

Serve warm or at room temperature.

❖

Tenderloin with Roquefort, Garlic Cream Sauce

Season the steaks liberally with salt and pepper and set aside, covered, at room temperature.

Rub the garlic with oil and bake until soft, about 25 minutes. Cool and remove the skins.

Purée the garlic with the cream and Roquefort.

Grill or sauté the steaks until cooked to the desired doneness.

In a sauté pan over low heat, combine the garlic cream with the brandy and dry vermouth. Simmer until the sauce is the desired consistency. Adjust seasonings. Drizzle sauce over steaks.

Trade Secret: The intense flavors of this dish are enhanced with a full-flavored red wine.

Serves 6
Preparation Time:
  30 Minutes
Pre-heat oven to 350°

6 filet mignons, 8 oz. each
  Salt and freshly ground
  black pepper
½ head garlic, unpeeled
2 Tbsps. oil
¾ cup heavy cream
¼ cup Roquefort cheese
3 Tbsps. brandy
3 Tbsps. dry vermouth

WARRINERS RESTAURANT

AMERICAN CUISINE
Box 407
Post Office Square
Edgartown
627-4488
Dinner 6PM–9PM
AVERAGE DINNER FOR TWO: $75

Owner Sam Warriner runs two restaurants under one roof. Warriners is a luxurious, reservations-only dining room in the library. Adjoining is the bistro-style Sam's, with a casual elegance where guests can wait at the bar to be seated and enjoy a less formal, no frills menu.

The cuisine in Warriners is regional American while the setting is English. The mahogany tables in the library are adorned with fine Dudson china (including matching vases and salt and pepper shakers), and small brass lamps. Soft lighting, Queen Anne chairs, fireplaces and a bookcase filled to the brim complete the home-like ambiance.

Honored with the 1989 award of excellence by Wine Spectator magazine, Warriners offers an excellent and extensive wine list. Impressively, there are about 150 wines to choose from—ranging in price from affordable to extravagant.

The menu is an ever-changing creative assortment of foods. Fresh fish of the day is announced and priced daily while other entrées like the seared Center Cut of Sirloin with Four Peppercorns and Thyme with Bass Ale Sauce can be found on the menu at any given time. The sautéed Cape Pogue Bay Scallops with a Melange of Radicchio, Endive and Spinach, or the Linguine and Lobster with Green Onions, Whiskey and Shallot Cream Sauce are two other possibilities. The desserts change daily as well and can include a decadent White Chocolate Mousse with Raspberries.

CHEF JIM KINGSLEY'S MENU FOR EIGHT

Salmon Gravlax with Tarragon Mustard Horseradish Sauce

Sautéed Scallops with Endive, Radicchio and Spinach

Salmon Gravlax

R inse salmon filet in cold water and pat dry with paper towel. Trim sides and ends if necessary so you have a nice rectangular piece.

Mix salt and sugar in a small bowl. Place filet on a large piece of plastic film, coat both sides of filet with sugar/salt mixture and wrap tightly with plastic film then wrap with foil. Place the salmon between two cookie sheets with at least 10 lbs. of weight on top and refrigerate for 24 hours.

Remove salmon from wrapping and rinse in cold water, pat dry and place on a piece of plastic wrap. Mix all the chopped herbs and divide into equal parts. Do the same with the zest and divide the cognac and black pepper in half. Then sprinkle ½ the ingredients over one side of the salmon in this order: cognac, black pepper, zest and herbs. Flip filet over on plastic wrap and repeat. Wrap lightly with plastic wrap, then foil, place between cookie sheets, press and refrigerate for another 24 hours.

The Tarragon Mustard Horseradish Sauce recipe follows.

Serves 8
Preparation Time:
1½ Hours
(note marinating time)

- 1 **lb. salmon filet with skin & pin bones removed**
- 2 **Tbsps. Kosher salt**
- 1 **Tbsp. brown sugar**
- ¼ **cup fresh parsley, chopped**
- 1½ **Tbsps. fresh oregano, chopped**
- 1½ **Tbsps. fresh sage, chopped**
- 1 **Tbsp. fresh thyme, chopped**
  Zest of ½ an orange
  Zest of ½ a lemon
  Zest of ½ a lime
- 1 **Tbsp. cognac**
- ½ **tsp. fresh black pepper, coarsely ground**

Tarragon Mustard Horseradish Sauce

Yields: 1 Cup
Preparation Time:
15 Minutes

- 2 **large egg yolks at room temperature**
- 1 **Tbsp. warm water**
- 1 **cup peanut oil**
- 1 **Tbsp. tarragon, chopped**
- ½ **tsp. honey**
- 2 **tsps. fresh lemon juice**
- 1½ **tsps. coarse grain mustard**
- 1½ **tsps. prepared horseradish**
- 3 **Tbsps. white wine**
- ½ **cup red onion, minced**
- ½ **cup capers, rinsed, drained**

lace the yolks and warm water in a food processor. Mix for 1 minute, then drizzle oil to make mayonnaise. If the mayonnaise becomes very thick, before adding oil, add the liquid ingredients.

Add the tarragon, honey, lemon juice, mustard and horseradish and mix well. Adjust consistency with white wine. Sauce should flow, but not be runny.

To serve over the salmon gravlax, slice the salmon thinly on a bias and arrange on a plate with minced red onion and capers, then dot plate with the sauce.

Sautéed Scallops with Radicchio, Endive and Spinach

To make the vinaigrette, combine the first five ingredients in a bowl, mix well and adjust any ingredient according to individual taste. Just keep in mind that the endive and radicchio are on the bitter side.

Remove the stems from the spinach, wash and let dry thoroughly. Cut the spinach into thin strips. Cut the radicchio in half, remove the core and julienne into thin strips. Do the same with the endive and mix all three in a bowl.

Rinse the scallops in water and remove the tough elastic muscle that attaches the scallops to the shell, and let them drain thoroughly.

Heat two very large sauté pans on the stove. Divide the butter and peanut oil between the two pans and let it reach the smoking point.

Carefully place the scallops in the pans, shake the pans vigorously and cook for about 1 minute. Do not overcook.

Add the julienne vegetables and sauté briefly. Now, with pans still on the heat, add the vinaigrette, salt and pepper and mix well. Remove from pans immediately and serve.

Serves 8
Preparation Time: One Hour

⅓ cup Balsamic vinegar
1 cup extra virgin olive oil
1 Tbsp. brown sugar
1 tsp. whole grain mustard
   Kosher salt & freshly ground white pepper to taste
2 bunches spinach
1 large head raddichio
2 heads Belgian endive
3 lbs. bay scallops
¾ cup clarified butter
¼ cup peanut oil

Nantucket

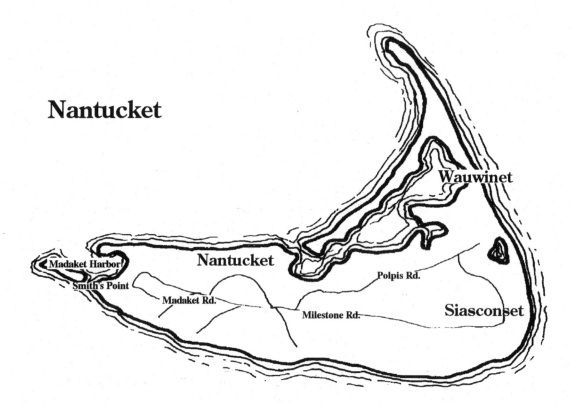

Wauwinet

Madaket Harbor

Nantucket

Smith's Point

Polpis Rd.

Madaket Rd.

Milestone Rd.

Siasconset

The nautical influence is so pervasive in Nantucket that even its shape is described in sea-going terms. Some insist that the island is shaped like a great whale flipping its tail. Others compare it to the curvature of a seaman's hammock.

The crescent-shaped island, about 30 miles long and 3½ miles at its widest point, takes its name from the Wampanoag Indian word, Nanticut, meaning "The Far-away Land." The Indians also called it Canopache, "The Place of Peace."

The Wampanoags had a fascinating legend about the formation of Nantucket. It seems that Nanina, a chief's beautiful daughter, was in love with Waposset, a poor warrior. Nanina's father refused to allow his daughter to marry a brave who owned no land.

In desperation, the young lovers appealed to Moshup, a legendary giant who lived on Martha's Vineyard. Moshup took pity on the lovers, picked them up and carried them to a confrontation with the chief. Even at the risk of angering the giant, the chief steadfastly refused to consent to the marriage because Waposset was so poor. With that, Moshup bade them all to follow him. He conjured up a storm and lit his pipe with a bolt of lightning. He calmly smoked the pipe, then knocked the ashes into the sea. Lo and behold, an island rose out of the sea. The giant took the lovers to the new land and told them it was theirs. The chief could no longer object, so Moshup married the couple. A great feast followed, of course. A more mundane version says that Nantucket was formed when Moshup threw his sand-filled moccasins out to sea.

One other Moshup legend points out how large he was. The Indians said that when Moshup was hungry, he would broil whole whales on the coals of huge trees which he pulled up by the roots.

The first written record of Nantucket was in 1605, when Capt. George Weymouth recorded seeing "a white, sandy cliff" 12 miles away from his ship. An attempt to land was made, but rough seas made that impossible. Credit for the first landing goes to English mariner Bartholomew Gosnold.

Nantucket was included in the royal grant to the Plymouth Company in 1621. The island was purchased in 1641 by Thomas Mayhew, who in 1659 sold nine-tenths of

NANTUCKET: Inside the Past

it to nine other men "for thirty pounds in good merchantable pay and two beaver hats, one for myself and one for my wife."

The new partners included Tristam Coffin, Thomas Macy, Christopher Hussey, Richard Swain, Thomas Barnard, Peter Coffin, Stephen Greenleaf, John Swain and William Pike. They, in turn, were allowed to choose one partner each. The new partners included Nathaniel and Edward Starbuck, Tristam Coffin Jr., Thomas Look, James Coffin, John Smith, Robert Barnard, Robert Pike and Thomas Coleman. These men formed the "Proprietors of the Common and Undivided Lands of Nantucket," an organization that still exists. You'll recognize these names all over the island.

But the proprietors did not move to the island right away. It took religious persecution to accomplish that.

The Puritans had control of the mainland, but they were intolerant of the up-and-coming Quakers, to the degree that they made it a crime to entertain Quakers. Thomas Macy, a Baptist, allowed some passing Quakers to find refuge from a storm in his house. When word of this infraction reached the Puritans, they fined Macy. Two of the men he had taken in were later hanged.

That did it. In the autumn of 1659, Macy, along with his wife and four children, plus Edward Starbuck and young Isaac Coleman, fled to Nantucket. They spent a lonely and bleak winter, but were joined by about 60 other settlers the following spring.

In time, the Quakers were to exert much influence on Nantucket. Their philosophy espoused pacifism and abstinence. They forbade music, dancing, books, the use of color—and even buttons. But while they lived in a drab world, they were hard-working and frugal. And they were natural-born whalers.

You see their influence throughout Nantucket, especially in the architecture and subdued colors. And their frugality included even speech. Hence we will see their shortened phrasing: 'Tucket for Nantucket, 'Sconset for Siasconset, and even the sperm whale's name was shortened from spermaceti whales.

Even today, the mention of Nantucket—anywhere in the world—brings whales to mind. At first, the whalers hunted right whales close to shore, just as the Indians

A whale captured close to shore is cut up on the beach. Indians showed the early settlers this technique.

Ship's figurehead adorns Nantucket house.

had. And the small whales were plentiful. But in 1712, Capt. Christopher Hussey was blown out to sea in a storm. He found himself amid a school of large whales, so he harpooned one and brought it back to Nantucket. It turned out to be a sperm whale, whose oil was more valuable than that of any other whales. The age of the deep-sea whaler had begun.

The establishment of the new industry brought with it great changes to Nantucket. The area known as the Great Harbor blossomed with warehouses and wharves. Soon ships laden with sperm whale oil were setting out to England. London at that time was infested with crime in the darkened streets, but the plentiful whale oil made street lights possible. When the crime rate went down, other cities saw the advantage of buying the whale oil. Sperm oil was the finest lubricant of its day and Nantucket thrived. Sailmakers, coopers, blacksmiths, carpenters and candle makers crowded the wharves.

By 1768, the town boasted 125 whaling ships and was the undisputed whaling capital of the world. The zeal of the whalers soon decimated the Atlantic whales, so the ships went further and further afield—all the way to the Pacific and the Arctic. It was profitable to go on such long voyages because an adult whale could contain as much as a ton of oil, to say nothing of the blubber and bones.

The whalers roamed the Pacific, enjoying the tropical paradises of Hawaii and the Fiji islands. It is said that 40 South Seas islands were discovered by the roving whalers.

Perhaps the greatest whaling saga of all time involved a Nantucket whaler in the Pacific. Capt. George Pollard of the ship Essex was thousands of miles from land in 1820, when a harpooned whale turned on a whaleboat, damaging it so badly it barely managed to return to the ship. Then the whale turned on the Essex, ramming it repeatedly until the ship began to sink. The crew managed to escape in three whaleboats.

But they were 2,000 miles from the nearest land. The boats became separated in a storm and two of the boats were never seen again. After weeks at sea, the intense heat, starvation and exposure began to take a heavy toll. The men were so desperate that when one of them died, the others would eat him. Soon they were reduced to casting lots to see who would be killed so that the others

*Weathervane on a
Nantucket House.*

*The dramatic
moment when
an early whaler
prepared to
harpoon
the whale.*

could eat. The emaciated survivors—including Captain Pollard—eventually landed in Chile and, in time, made it back to Nantucket. The chilling story was the inspiration for Herman Melville's classic, "Moby Dick."

One other note in passing: Nantucket will forever be memorialized in the annals of whaling by the term "Nantucket sleighride." That was the unbelievable moment when the whale, enraged by the pain of the harpoon stuck in him, would flee, pulling the whaleboat and its crew after him in a heart-pounding ride. It was said that whalers paid "a drop of blood for every drop of oil."

Today, Nantucket offers an inside view into the past. The town of Nantucket, with its cobblestone streets and brick sidewalks, contains hundreds of authentic homes from the 18th and 19th centuries. Indeed, the aura of olden times is easy to see.

Some of the sights include the Whaling Museum, housed in a former sperm candle factory; the Peter Folger Museum, which covers the island's history; the Maria Mitchell Observatory, where an early woman was the first to spot a new comet; the Oldest House, built in 1686; the Old Jail (they still spell in the Old Gaol), built in 1805; and The Old Mill, circa 1746, the entire top assembly of which can be turned to face the wind.

Main Street and its environs boasts 400 houses built before 1850. Among the most noteworthy are the Three Bricks and the Two Greeks. Thomas Starbuck built three strikingly beautiful Georgian-style houses for his three sons, but the canny old whaling merchant did not allow the sons to take possession until they had entered the family business. Across the street are the two white-pillared Greek Revival masterpieces. William Hadwen built the first one for himself and the second as a home for his niece. Today one of the homes, the Hadwen-Satler memorial, is open to the public for tours.

Other parts of the island are beautiful as well. The Eastern shores contain popular summer communities: Wauwinet, Squam, Quidnet and Siasconset (make sure you call it 'Sconset). The southern shore contains the hamlet of Surfside and the western shore contains the village of Madaket.

Away from the settlements, one finds the peaceful beauty of sand dunes, rolling moors, arrays of wildflowers, pine and oak groves, swamps and cranberry bogs.

And, of course, the most important asset of the islands—the eternal sea. Everything in Nantucket has ties to the sea and beyond. In fact, you'll see a sign in 'Sconset that says: "3,000 miles to Spain."

Explore the unique island of Nantucket and you will smell and feel and experience the pages of this nation's history. But more than that, you will be better able to understand the people who created America. ❖

Vacationers on Oak Bluffs Beach, circa 1910.

AMERICAN SEASONS

AMERICAN CUISINE
80 Centre Street
Nantucket Island
228-7111
Dinner 6PM–10PM
AVERAGE DINNER FOR TWO: $60

Off the beaten path, this intimate restaurant offers exciting regional cuisine at affordable prices. The menu offers a wide diversity of food, including New England, Down South, Wild West and Pacific Coast selections. The 50-seat dining room was redecorated in 1991 and now includes American folk art, old murals and tables with hand painted gameboards on them. Owners Linda and Everett Reid III have created a relaxed, entertaining atmosphere.

A guest can be a culinary traveler across the U.S. by sampling an entrée from the Wild West like grilled Rocky Mountain Wild Trout with a sauce of roasted chilis and sweet corn, or from the Pacific Coast by trying the Confit of Duckling with Wild Rice with Northwest Huckleberries. Let's not forget entrées from New England and Down South. Nantucket Lobster and Wild Mushroom Pancake with American Golden Caviar, or Grilled Maine Scallops with Spring Asparagus Sauce of Lemon and Leeks exemplify New England seafood. A guest can sample Southern cuisine with an appetizer of Grilled Country Sausage with "Cowgirl" Beans and Biscuits, or an entrée of Oven Roasted Buttermilk Chicken with Red Beans and Rice with a Smoky Remoulade.

CHEF EVERETT REID III'S MENU FOR FOUR

Lobster & Wild Mushroom Pancakes with Crème Fraîche

Grilled Venison in Smoked Tomato Barbecue Sauce

Lobster & Wild Mushroom Pancakes

n olive oil, sauté the garlic and shallots and set aside. Sauté the wild mushrooms in olive oil and set aside.

In a large mixing bowl, combine the eggs, milk and butter. Slowly stir in the flour, mixing well. Add the garlic and shallots.

Lightly grease a skillet with oil and place it over medium heat. Drop the batter by tablespoons to form 5″ pancakes onto the hot griddle. Place the lobster meat, wild mushrooms, scallions, and seasonings on top of each pancake. Turn when the pancake tops are bubbling and the undersides are golden brown. Continue cooking for 2 minutes over low heat.

Serve immediately. Garnish with crème fraîche, golden caviar, and fresh chives.

Serves 4
Preparation Time:
30 Minutes

Olive oil
1 garlic clove, minced
1 shallot, minced
2 cups wild mushrooms, sliced
2 eggs
1½ cups milk
1 Tbsp. melted butter
2 cups all-purpose flour, sifted
1 tsp. corn oil
2 lobsters, grilled, meat removed, diced
1 scallion, chopped
Kosher salt & cracked black pepper to taste
Crème fraîche
Golden caviar, garnish
Chives, chopped, garnish

❖

Grilled Venison in Smoked Tomato Barbecue Sauce

Serves 4
Preparation Time:
   15 Minutes
(note marinating time)

  4 **venison steaks**
    (about 2 lbs. total)
  1 **cup olive oil**
  ½ **cup white wine vinegar**
  4 **cloves garlic, coarsely**
    chopped
  2 **bay leaves**
    Cracked pepper to taste
    Barbecue sauce, recipe
    follows

T rim the venison steaks of excess fat. Place the steaks in a shallow roasting pan.

Combine the oil, vinegar, garlic, bay leaves and pepper in a small bowl. Stir well, and pour over the steaks. Cover the pan, and marinate in the refrigerator, turning occasionally, for up to 6 hours.

Brush each steak liberally with the barbecue sauce. Grill the meat by searing the steaks quickly over medium heat on each side. Then cook an additional 2 to 3 minutes per side for rare meat, 4 to 5 minutes for medium.

Tomato Barbecue Sauce

I n a large stock pot, sauté the onions and garlic in oil until soft. Add the remaining ingredients, stirring thoroughly. Bring to a boil. Reduce heat and gently simmer on low heat for 2 hours, stirring frequently. Purée in a food processor. Adjust seasonings to taste.

Yields: 2 cups
Preparation Time:
  2½ Hours

3 onions, finely diced
1 head of garlic, chopped
  fine
¼ cup corn oil
8 tomatoes, chopped
1 cup red wine vinegar
¼ cup brown sugar
2 Tbsps. Dijon mustard
3 jalapeños, chopped
3 chipotle peppers, dried
  Salt and pepper to taste
  Chile powder to taste
  Tabasco to taste
  Cumin to taste

❖

THE BOARDING HOUSE

INTERNATIONAL CUISINE
12 Federal Street
Nantucket
228-9622
Lunch Noon–2:30PM
Dinner 6PM–9:30PM
AVERAGE DINNER FOR TWO: $80

T he Boarding House is a local favorite. Food is served in the cathedral ceilinged Victorian lounge at marble-top tables or in the sunken dining room. The dining room is romantic with gentle lighting, low ceilings, exposed beams and a mural. The walls are plaster and brick and add to the rustic ambiance.

Seth Raynor, the owner and executive chef makes international cuisine with a contemporary flair. Entrée highlights are a Roast Pork Chop with Braised Cabbage and Juniper Berry Jus, and a Grilled Chicken Risotto with Roasted Onions and Thyme Jus. Appetizers include Tempura Fried Calamari and Shrimp with Lemon Basil Aioli, and Sautéed Crab Cakes with Roasted Jalapeño Crème Fraîche. One delectable finale is Chef Raynor's Chocolate Bourbon Terrine with Maple Crème Anglaise. The terrine is made more irresistible with a garnish of chocolate sauce.

CHEF SETH C. RAYNOR'S MENU FOR SIX

Lacquered Shrimp with Thai Pesto Noodles

Roasted Salmon in Buerre Rouge

Chocolate Bourbon Terrine with Maple Crème Anglaise

Lacquered Shrimp with Thai Pesto Noodles

Place garlic, basil, mint, cilantro, both oils, chili sauce, water, salt and pepper to taste in a food processor until the pesto is puréed. Do not over-process or color will fade.

Drain and rinse the capellini under cold water and toss with the pesto.

Top each serving with 5 grilled shrimp. Drizzle with the Soy Ginger Glaze (recipe follows).

Serves 6
Preparation Time:
  30 Minutes

  6 garlic cloves, peeled
  1 cup fresh basil leaves
  ½ cup fresh mint leaves
  ½ cup fresh cilantro
  ½ cup canola oil
  1 Tbsp. sesame oil
  2 Tbsps. Thai chile sauce
  2 Tbps. water
     Salt to taste
  2 lbs. capellini pasta, cooked
 30 shrimp, grilled

❖

Soy Ginger Glaze

Serves 6
Preparation Time:
  One Hour

- ½ cup hoisin
- ⅓ cup + 3 Tbsps. soy sauce
- ⅔ cup brown sugar
- 2 garlic cloves, peeled
- 2 Tbsps. fresh ginger, peeled, roughly chopped
- 2 star anise
- 2 dried Chinese red chiles
- ¼ cup rice wine vinegar
- 2 cups water
- ¼ cup cornstarch
- 1 Tbsp. Wasabi powder
- ¼ tsp. 5 spice powder

Place the hoisin, ⅓ cup soy sauce and brown sugar in a saucepan over low heat.

Purée the garlic, ginger, anise, red chiles, wine vinegar and water in a blender for 30 seconds until smooth. Add the blended ingredients to the ingredients in the saucepan and simmer for 20 minutes. Remove from heat and steep for one hour.

Mix the cornstarch, Wasabi powder, 5 spice powder and 3 Tbsps. soy sauce. Bring the steeped ingredients back to a boil and slowly add the Wasabi mix and simmer for two to three minutes. Strain through fine sieve.

Roasted Salmon with Beurre Rouge

Season the filets with salt and pepper. In a hot sauté pan, add 2 Tbsps. canola oil and cook the filets, top down, for three minutes. Flip, remove pan from heat, and cook the bottom for one minute, then remove filets.

Place shallots, wine and thyme in heavy non-reactive saucepan and reduce to almost dry. Add the cream and reduce to syrupy consistency. Slowly add butter, little by little, whisking constantly. Do not boil. Season with salt and pepper.

Trade Secret: Serve with cabbage and caramelized shallots.

Serves 6
Preparation Time:
  30 Minutes

  6 salmon filets, 6 oz. each
     Salt and pepper
  2 Tbsps. canola oil
  ⅓ cup shallots, finely
     minced
  1 cup red wine
  ⅛ tsp. fresh thyme leaves
  1 Tbsp. heavy cream
  8 Tbsps. (1 stick) butter

❖

Chocolate Bourbon Terrine with Maple Crème Anglaise

Serves 6
Preparation Time:
  45 Minutes
(note refrigeration time)
Pre-heat oven to 425°

½ lb. bittersweet
  chocolate, shaved
¼ lb. butter
 1 oz. bourbon
 3 eggs
 2 Tbsps. sugar

Melt the chocolate and butter in a double boiler. Add the bourbon to the chocolate and set aside.
Whip the eggs and sugar in a double boiler until the volume triples. Fold egg mix into chocolate mix.

Pour the mixture into 4 oz. ramekins sprayed with vegetable spray. Bake in water bath with towel on bottom uncovered for five minutes and remove. Place foil over ramekins and bake for 10 minutes, then cool at room temperature for 45 minutes. Refrigerate. Maple Crème Anglaise recipe follows.

❖

Maple Crème Anglaise

Scald the milk and vanilla, then remove from heat. Mix the yolks and ¼ cup sugar and add to the milk. Add the maple syrup and cook over a double boiler until the mixture coats the back of a spoon. Strain and cool.

To assemble, unmold the Chocolate Bourbon Terrine and pour Crème Anglaise over it.

Trade Secret: For added decadence, garnish with chocolate sauce.

Yields: 3 cups

2 cups milk
¼ tsp. vanilla
6 egg yolks
¼ cup sugar
3 Tbsps. maple syrup

❖

THE CHANTICLEER

FRENCH CUISINE
9 New Street
Siasconset, Nantucket
257-6231
Lunch Noon–2:30PM
Dinner 6:30PM–12:30AM
AVERAGE DINNER FOR TWO: $120

Within this rose-covered cottage is one of the island's finest restaurants. Lunch in the rose garden is a local tradition, as is an after-dinner drink in the bar. Both a five-course prix-fixe menu and a la carte menu are available at dinner. The extraordinary wine cellar, which has won the Wine Spectator Grand Award, offers 900 selections of California and French wines.

For two decades, owner-chef Jean-Charles Berruet has created elegant classic-French feasts, prepared like nothing else you've ever experienced. Using fresh local ingredients and herbs, his characteristic dishes include an appetizer of Escargot and Hazelnut-filled Raviolis, served in a Sweet Garlic Broth followed by Scaloppini of Salmon sauté with a Dry Vermouth, Sorrel and Cream Sauce, or an entree of Baby Chicken stuffed with Mushrooms, Herbs and Ricotta, roasted and served with a mild Vinegar Sauce and Wild Rice Risotto. Tempting desserts range from very thin slices of Granny Smith Apples on a thin layer of Puff Pastry, cooked to order, an assortment of fresh Sorbets or Chocolate Decadence served with an Espresso Sauce.

Dining at The Chanticleer is like being a privileged guest in the finest private home.

CHEF JEAN-CHARLES BERRUET'S MENU FOR FOUR

Cream of Asparagus Soup

Chicken Stuffed with Herbs

in a Mild Vinegar Sauce

Chocolate Decadence with Espresso Sauce

Cream of Asparagus Soup

Open the oysters, save and strain the liquid. Set aside.

Clean the asparagus and cut 2″ off each bottom. Cut the tips off the asparagus, setting aside the base. Cook the asparagus tips in boiling water or steam making sure to leave the asparagus slightly crisp. Remove from heat and cool.

In a large heavy soup pot, combine the milk and water, bring to a boil. Chop the remaining asparagus stems and cook them in the milk until tender.

Purée the asparagus stem mixture in the blender or food processor until smooth. Strain into another pot, add the cream, bring to a boil, add the butter, then thicken with corn starch.

Bring the oyster liquid to a boil. Cook the oysters for one minute, remove the oysters from the broth and add the broth to the soup. Season with white pepper and nutmeg; salt may not be needed.

To serve, fill each soup bowl and garnish with warm asparagus tips and oysters.

Serves 4
Preparation Time:
  One Hour

24 **Oysters**
 2 **bunches asparagus**
 1 **qt. milk**
 1 **cup water**
 ½ **cup cream**
 4 **Tbsps. (½ stick)**
    unsalted butter
 2 **tsps. corn starch**
    White pepper to taste
    Nutmeg to taste

❖

Chicken Stuffed With Herbs In a Mild Vinegar Sauce

Serves 4
Preparation Time:
   30 Minutes
Pre-heat oven to 400°

- 4 baby chickens or game hens, about 1 lb. each
- 2 Tbsps. unsalted butter
- ½ lb. pancetta
   Juice of 1 lemon
- 1 Tbsp. water
- 4 Tbsps. parsley, chopped
- 1 Tbsp. chives, chopped
- 1 tsp. tarragon, chopped
- ½ lb. mushrooms
- 1 cup ricotta cheese
- 4 shallots, chopped
- 1 Tbsp. red wine vinegar
- ½ cup chicken stock
- 3 Tbsps. heavy cream
- 1 small tomato, peeled, seeded, chopped fine
- 1 tsp. chervil, optional

I n a food processor, process together the butter, pancetta, lemon juice and water for one minute. Add the parsley, chives, tarragon, mushrooms, ricotta, and 3 of the shallots. Process until mixture has the consistency of a paste.

Take each chicken and starting from the neck side, very carefully lift the skin from the body with your fingers. Make sure you don't puncture the skin or remove it completely. Take some stuffing and carefully push it in the space between the skin and the flesh. Pay special attention to the breast and the legs.

Place the birds in a roasting pan. Cook for 10 minutes in the oven at 400° and then for 25 minutes at 350.°

Remove the chicken from the pan and discard any fat. Add the last shallot and cook for one minute. Deglaze the pan with vinegar and reduce. Add the chicken stock and the cream. Bring to a boil and allow the sauce to cook for a minute or two. Add the tomato and chervil.

Trade Secret: A wild rice risotto or fresh pasta makes a wonderful accompaniment.

Chocolate Decadence in Espresso Sauce

In a double boiler over low heat, melt the chocolate. Remove from heat.

In a large mixing bowl, combine 7 egg yolks and 1¼ cups sugar, whipping together until fluffy. Slowly incorporate the melted chocolate, gently lifting up the mixture with a wooden spatula to make it light and airy.

In a separate bowl, work the butter with a fork, until soft and smooth. Add the cocoa powder, a small amount at a time, until well blended. Add the cocoa butter to the chocolate. Fold in the whipped cream and blend thoroughly. Set aside in a cool place.

Soak the ladyfingers in cold espresso. Line the bottom and sides of a terrine mold with parchment paper then with the ladyfingers. Fill the mold with the chocolate mix. Refrigerate overnight.

To make the espresso sauce, bring ¼ cup sugar and 2 cups milk to a boil over high heat, add the espresso grounds, cover the pot and let brew for 15 minutes.

Whisk 6 egg yolks and ¼ cups sugar in a bowl; whip until fluffy. Add the coffee infusion, mix well, and cook over low heat until the mixture has thickened slightly and coats the back of a metal spoon. Do not allow the sauce to boil or it will curdle.

Serve warm or at room temperature over the chocolate decadence.

Serves 4
Preparation Time:
  One Hour
(note refrigeration time)

  5 oz. semi-sweet
     chocolate
 13 egg yolks
 1¾ cups sugar
 16 Tbsps. (2 sticks)
     unsalted butter
 ¾ cup cocoa powder
  1 cup cream, whipped
 24 ladyfingers
  1 cup espresso coffee,
     cold
  2 cups milk
  2 tsps. ground espresso

❖

THE CLUB CAR

CONTINENTAL CUISINE
1 Main Street
Nantucket
228-1101
Lunch and Dinner 11 AM–1 AM
AVERAGE DINNER FOR TWO: $55

The restaurant is named after the railway car—one that ran from Steamboat Wharf to 'Sconset years ago. A lively cocktail piano lounge is now housed in this red train car. Beyond is an expansive dining room decorated with hanging plants, upholstered cane-back chairs, soft lighting, linen and silver.

The continental menu, which changes often, features fresh local seafoods and prime meats. First courses may include squid in the style of Bangkok with hot Asian spices or cream of chanterelle soup, tangy with onion and herbs. Entrée choices such as grilled medallions of fresh salmon with caviar custard and light lobster sauce or a rack of lamb glazed with honey mustard and herbs or a galantine of veal with pistachios and truffles are among the possibilities. Finish with one of a dozen desserts such as fresh berries with Devon cream or chocolate mousse cake with crème anglaise.

CHEF MICHAEL SHANNON'S MENU FOR FOUR

Squid with Hot Asian Spices

Sweetbreads Grand Marnier with Ginger

Chocolate Almond Macaroons

Squid with Hot Asian Spices

Wash squid. Peel membrane, take out cartilage, and slice into rings.

Heat a large sauté pan until very hot. Add squid and move around so that the squid cooks evenly, about 30 seconds. Remove from heat.

Place squid in a bowl over ice. When chilled, mix with the remaining ingredients. Adjust seasonings to your taste.

Serves 4
Preparation Time:
   15 Minutes
(note refrigeration time)

1 lb. squid
1 Tbsp. lime juice
1 Tbsp. Thai fish sauce
2 tsps. mint, chopped
2 tsps. cilantro, chopped
1 tsp. hot peppers, diced fine
1 cup tomato, seeded, peeled, diced
1 cup scallions, chopped
2 Tbsps. catsup

❖

Sweetbreads Grand Marnier with Ginger

Serves 4
Preparation Time:
 45 Minutes
(note refrigeration time)

 2 lbs. sweetbreads
1½ qts. water
 1 cup white wine
 4 Tbsps. vinegar
 1 celery, roughly
   chopped
 1 onion, roughly
   chopped
 1 Tbsp. pickling spice
   Juice of 1 lemon
 3 bay leaves
 6 peppercorns
 1 cup flour
 2 Tbsps. sweet butter
 4 Tbsps. shallots,
   chopped
½ cup Grand Marnier
 2 tsps. pepper
 2 tsps. honey
   Juice and zest of
   1 orange
 8 slices fresh ginger
 2 tsps. ginger preserves
 1 cup veal or beef stock
 2 tsps. green
   peppercorns
 2 Tbsps. crystallized
   ginger

Blanch sweetbreads in a bouillon base made of water, white wine, 2 Tbsps. vinegar, celery, onion, pickling spice, lemon, bay leaves and peppercorns for approximately 5 to 8 minutes until cooked rare. Cool in ice water a few minutes to stop cooking. Clean membranes. Press sweetbreads between 2 clean towels and sheet pans with weights on top overnight. Refrigerate.

Slice sweetbreads on the bias ½" thick. Lightly flour sweetbreads and sauté in butter. Brown on both sides and sweat shallots. Do not brown shallots. Deglaze pan with Grand Marnier. Add pepper, 2 Tbsps. vinegar, honey, juice of orange, fresh ginger and ginger preserves. Reduce until mixture forms into a light syrup. Add veal or beef stock to desired consistency.

To serve, strain sauce and pour over sweetbreads. Garnish with green peppercorns, crystallized ginger and orange zest.

Chocolate Almond Macaroons

Melt chocolate in a double boiler. Remove from heat when chocolate has melted.

Beat egg whites with cream of tartar to firm peaks. Gradually beat in sugar, a ¼ cup at a time. Add egg yolk and blend.

Fold a third of the egg whites into the chocolate to lighten. Blend in almonds, then fold in remaining egg whites.

Place cookie mix into pastry bag or spoon onto greased cookie sheet 1″ apart. Bake for 4 to 5 minutes until cookies puff and edges are slightly wrinkled. Remove from oven and cool.

Yields: 36 cookies
Preparation Time:
   30 Minutes
Preheat Oven to 400°

6 oz. bittersweet
   chocolate
4 egg whites
¼ tsp. cream of tartar
1 egg yolk
¾ cup sugar
½ cup almonds, chopped
   fine

❖

THE GALLEY ON CLIFFSIDE BEACH

MEDITERRANEAN CUISINE
19 Jefferson Avenue
Nantucket
228-9641
Lunch Noon–2PM
Dinner 6:30PM–10PM
AVERAGE DINNER FOR TWO: $70

T he Galley Restaurant on Cliffside Beach is the only Nantucket restaurant where you can enjoy a beachfront patio overlooking 100 feet of manicured, white sand beach and the alluring Atlantic. The patio is filled with wicker chairs, tables draped in blue and white tablecloths, and hanging planters with brightly colored flowers. The restaurant is a refined French bistro serving fresh Nantucket seafood with a Mediterranean flare.

Lunch at The Galley feels like dining at an exclusive private beach club while dinner offers a romantic experience. Romance blooms here with live piano music, flickering candlelight and the setting sun over the sea.

CHEF DANIEL FOUQUENOT'S MENU FOR SIX

Calamari Salad

Paella

Poached Pears in Raspberry Syrup

Calamari Salad

Bring 2 qts. of water to a boil with 1 tsp. salt. Plunge the calamari into boiling water for 1 minute. Drain and rinse under cold water. Squeeze lemon over cooled calamari.

In a large mixing bowl, combine the remaining ingredients. Refrigerate overnight.

Serve on bed of crisp greens and garnish as desired.

Serves 6
Preparation Time:
  20 Minutes
(note refrigeration time)

  2 qts. water
  2 lbs. calamari, cleaned,
     rinsed and cut
     in ¼" pieces
  1 lemon
  1 bunch scallions, finely
     chopped
  ½ medium red onion,
     diced
  2 stalks celery, finely
     diced
  ½ red pepper, diced
  ½ green pepper, diced
  4 garlic cloves, finely
     chopped
  ½ cup Italian parsley,
     chopped
  1 cup light virgin olive oil
  ½ cup Balsamic vinegar
  1 tsp. herbs de Provence
  1 tsp. red pepper flakes
     Salt and pepper to taste

Paella

Serves 8
Preparation Time:
One Hour

12 **pieces chicken, skinned**
½ **cup olive oil**
3 **cloves garlic, chopped**
1 **cup onion, chopped**
½ **cup green peppers,**
   chopped
½ **cup red peppers,**
   chopped
3 **cups rice**
½ **tsp. saffron**
½ **tsp. herbs de Provence**
¼ **tsp. red pepper flakes**
1 **lb. chorizo, sliced**
   in ½" pieces
2 **cups clam juice**
5 **cups chicken stock**
½ **cup peas, frozen or fresh**
½ **cup artichoke hearts,**
   frozen or fresh
½ **cup chick peas, canned**
1 **Tbsp. pimento strips**
24 **mussels**
24 **small clams**
24 **medium-large shrimp**
   Salt and pepper to taste
½ **cup parsley, chopped**
   Heavy large, round pan

F lour chicken pieces and sauté in olive oil until brown. Set aside.

Combine garlic, onion, red and green peppers, and sauté until soft, not browned. Add the rice and sauté for 2 minutes. Add saffron, herbs, red pepper flakes, chorizo and chicken. Pour in clam juice and chicken stock. Lower heat and simmer 10 minutes. Add peas, artichoke hearts and simmer 5 more minutes. Add chick peas and pimento strips. Stir around a bit to arrange evenly and attractively.

Meanwhile, steam mussels and clams until open. Keep warm. Arrange shrimp on top of paella for the last 5 minutes of cooking or until they are bright pink. Remember to test rice. Liquid should be absorbed. Arrange clams and mussels on top. Cover with chopped parsley. Serve in the pan.

Trade Secret: The chef often finishes off the paella in the oven.

Poached Pears in Raspberry Syrup

ombine sugar with 3 cups water. Boil. Stir to dissolve the sugar. Add the lemon rinds and simmer for 10 minutes.

Purée the raspberries. Stir the purée into the syrup and remove from heat.

Peel the pears and scoop out the blossom ends. Add to the syrup, simmer and turn occasionally. Cook until tender but not soft, 30 to 35 minutes. Boil the sauce, adding the Framboise.

Transfer the pears to a shallow dish and cool covered for 2 to 3 hours. Strain the cool syrup over the pears. Serve with crème fraîche or soft whipped cream.

Serves 6
Preparation Time:
   45 Minutes

1 cup sugar
2 lemon rinds, 3″ long
1 cup frozen raspberries
6 Bosc pears
1 oz. Framboise liqueur
   Crème fraîche or soft
   whipped cream

INDIA HOUSE

ECLECTIC CUISINE
37 India Street
Nantucket
228-9043
Dinner 6:30PM–9:30PM
AVERAGE DINNER FOR TWO: $50

India House, an attractive, authentic, turn of the eighteenth century inn, offers an exceptional dining experience. Bountiful gourmet breakfasts are served in the outdoor garden cafe. Freshly squeezed orange juice and home-made breads and muffins preface creatively prepared entrees such as soft shell crab stuffed with scallop mousse or blueberry-stuffed French toast.

Dinner is served in one of the three romantic dining rooms. Candlelight, crisp linen and abundant fresh flowers set the mood for the glorious cuisine to follow. Fresh Nantucket seafood and Lamb India House are but two of the acclaimed specialties. India House offers a good selection of French and domestic wines, as well as cocktails.

CHEF MICHAEL CARACCIDO'S MENU FOR FOUR

Stuffed Calamari in Pesto Cream Sauce

Pecan Cashew Glazed Swordfish

Coffee Ice Cream Truffles with Hazelnuts

Stuffed Calamari in Pesto Cream Sauce

Clean the calamari tubes and leave whole. Refrigerate.

Prepare the stuffing by cooking the rice in boiling water with the olive oil, bouquet garni, and salt. Cook until slightly overdone, approximately 45 minutes. Rinse with cold water, strain and set aside.

In a sauté pan, sweat the shallots and garlic for one minute. Add the shrimp, capers, parsley, fish stock, lemon juice and white wine. Cook for one minute, remove from heat and cool. Process stuffing in a food processor to desired texture.

With a piping bag or spoon, fill calamari tubes three quarters of the way full with stuffing. Tie the end with a cotton string.

In a large sauté pan over medium high heat, brown the stuffed calamari tubes. Add the tentacles, cooking for 2 minutes. Remove from heat.

Prepare the pesto cream sauce by combining the pesto and wine in a small saucepan over low heat. Add the heavy cream and reduce until the sauce coats the back of a spoon.

To serve, place stuffed calamari on a pool of pesto cream sauce. Remove strings and garnish with tentacles and chopped basil.

Serves 4
Preparation Time:
  One Hour

- 1 **lb. calamari tubes with tentacles**
- 2 **cups rice**
- 4 **cups water**
- ¼ **cup olive oil**
  Bouquet garni, optional
  Salt and pepper to taste
- 3 **large shallots, peeled, chopped**
- 2 **garlic cloves, peeled, chopped**
- ½ **lb. shrimp, peeled, grilled, chopped**
- 2 **Tbsps. capers**
- ⅓ **cup parsley, chopped fine**
- 3 **Tbsps. fish stock**
  Juice of half lemon
- 3 **Tbsps. white wine**
  Cotton string to secure calamari tubes
- ⅓ **cup basil pesto**
- ¼ **cup dry white wine**
- ⅓ **cup heavy cream**
  Basil, chopped for garnish

❖

Pecan Cashew Glazed Swordfish

Serves 4
Preparation Time:
45 Minutes
Pre-heat oven to 450°

4 swordfish steaks
1 cup roasted cashews,
   unsalted
1 cup pecans
⅔ cup light brown sugar
   Juice of half lime
   Freshly ground pepper
   to taste
½ cup olive oil
1 small red onion,
   chopped fine
½ cup granulated sugar
4 sprigs fresh thyme
   Juice of 1 lime
1¼ cups Rose's lime juice

I n a food processor, combine nuts and process until finely chopped. Place in a mixing bowl and add the brown sugar, lime, pepper and olive oil. Mix the nut glaze with your hands until you can make a tight ball. Cover each steak with the glaze, pressing down to create an even topping. Set aside while preparing the sauce.

In a saucepan, combine the onion, granulated sugar, thyme and lime juice, bringing the mixture to a boil. Reduce the heat and cook until the sauce is red, glossy and will cling to a spoon. Remove from heat and keep warm.

Roast steaks at 450° until the nuts have browned, approximately 7 to 10 minutes. Top each steak with a small amount of the caramelized red onion sauce.

❖

Coffee Ice Cream Truffles with Hazelnuts

I n a double boiler, melt the chocolate and butter until incorporated, stirring occasionally. Add the cream and Kahlua. Just before the mixture begins to boil, remove from heat and let stand at room temperature.

Form a small round ball of ice cream with a fruit scoop. Dip in chocolate sauce and roll in the chopped nuts. Place on a holding plate covered with wax paper until ready to serve. Freeze at least 1 hour before serving.

Trade Secret: Experiment with variations using chopped white and dark chocolate chunks, Dutch cocoa powder, Frangelico and macadamia nuts.

Serves 8
Preparation Time:
  45 Minutes
(note refrigeration time)

16 oz. dark unsweetened
    chocolate
16 Tbsps. (2 sticks)
    unsalted butter
½ cup heavy cream
 2 oz. Kahlua
 2 pts. coffee ice cream
 2 cups roasted hazelnuts,
    coarsely chopped

JARED COFFIN HOUSE

AMERICAN CUISINE
29 Broad Street
Nantucket
228-2400
Dinner 6:30PM–9PM
AVERAGE DINNER FOR TWO: $70

Jared's, the signature restaurant of the Jared Coffin House, is found on the first floor of the house built in 1845. The three-story brick building was the first of its kind to be built on Nantucket and houses a unique restaurant. The casually elegant dining room is decorated with salmon colored walls, Federal period antique furniture and chandeliers. The dining room is elegant but comfortable and offers creative American cuisine and old New England favorites prepared in imaginative new ways.

The menu changes seasonally with a strong emphasis on seafood. Summer entrées include a Poached Salmon served with Cucumbers and a yogurt dill sauce, and a Trio of Lamb with a Pecan Crusted Rack, Sliced Leg of Lamb and Lamb Sausage with a Cabernet Glaze. Local Haddock Sautéed with Spinach and a yellow pepper sauce and a Country Roasted Pork with Cranberry Stuffing and a Port Wine Glaze are two other seasonal delights.

Appetizers and salads are unique and plentiful with Crab and Corn Cakes with a Sweet Red Pepper Marmalade, and an unusual salad of smoked fresh mozarella with local tomatoes and a Chianti vinaigrette. The desserts include such indulgent treats as a Bailey's Chocolate Paté with a Crème Anglaise and on Christmas Eve, a Pumpkin Cheesecake with Gingersnap Crust.

CHEF WENDY MARTIN'S MENU FOR EIGHT

Bay Scallops on the Half Shell

Nantucket Blue Salad with Blueberry Vinaigrette

Lobster Bisque

Bay Scallops on the Half Shell

To make the marinade, mix together the yellow mustard, dry mustard, ¾ cup olive oil, sugar, vinegar, Tabasco, Worcestershire sauce and salt in a food processor until thoroughly combined.

Refrigerate until served.

Toss the scallops in the vermouth, Pernod, ¼ cup olive oil, garlic, dill, lemon zest and peppercorns in a glass bowl. Refrigerate at least 3 hours, but no longer than 24 hours.

Pre-heat the broiler. For each hors d'oeuvre, place 2 scallops in the center of a scallop shell. Spoon a bit of the marinade over the scallop.

Place the shells on a baking sheet. Broil 6″ from the heat just until the scallops are tender and cooked, about 3 minutes. Serve in the shells.

Serves 8
Preparation Time:
  One Hour
(note marinating time)

27 oz. prepared yellow
   mustard
12 oz. dry mustard
 1 cup olive oil
4½ cups sugar
1½ cups cider vinegar
 6 drops Tabasco
 2 Tbsps. Worcestershire
   sauce
 2 Tbsps. salt
 1 lb. bay scallops
 3 Tbsps. vermouth
 2 Tbsps. Pernod
 1 Tbsp. garlic, chopped
 2 Tbsps. fresh dill,
   chopped
 1 tsp. lemon zest
 1 Tbsp. green
   peppercorns

❖

Nantucket Blue Salad
with Blueberry Vinaigrette

Serves 8
Preparation Time:
  15 Minutes

2½ **cups fresh blueberries**
1½ **lbs. spinach**
12 **oz. bleu cheese,**
     crumbled
 ½ **cup pecan halves,**
     lightly toasted
 ¾ **cup rice wine vinegar**
 ¼ **cup raspberry vinegar**
 1 **cup olive oil**

Rinse and drain blueberries. Wash and dry the spinach, tearing it into bite-sized pieces. Divide spinach among 8 salad plates. Place 3 Tbsps. blueberries, 3 Tbsps. bleu cheese and ½ ounce toasted pecans on each serving.

For the blueberry vinaigrette, place vinegars and 1 cup blueberries in a blender and process until smooth. Slowly add the olive oil until all the ingredients are combined.

Top salad with vinaigrette.

Lobster Bisque

Break up lobster bodies with mallet. In large pot, heat 3 Tbsps. oil until smoking, add lobster shells and sear, stirring for 15–20 minutes. Add diced onion, carrots, and celery and cook until the onions and carrots are golden brown around the edges. Add tomato paste, cook until paste goes from red to brick color and looks dry. Add brandy, clam juice and water. Cook until liquid is reduced by half. Add cream and half & half. Bring back to a simmer.

Strain out shells and other solids, pressing down to extract as much liquid as possible.

In separate pot, melt the butter. Stir in flour until smooth. Slowly add bisque, whisking constantly to avoid lumps. Bring soup to a simmer, season with salt and pepper and keep warm until served.

Garnish with diced lobster meat and chopped fresh parsley.

Serves 8
Preparation Time:
  30 Minutes

  2 lbs. lobsters
  3 Tbsps. cooking oil
  1 yellow onion,
    large dice
  2 carrots, diced
  3 stalks celery, diced
  1 small can tomato paste
  ½ cup brandy
  1 pt. clam juice
  1 cup water
1½ pts. heavy cream
  1 qt. half & half
  4 Tbsps. butter (½ stick)
  ½ cup flour
    Salt and pepper

❖

LE LANGUEDOC

AMERICAN AND CONTINENTAL CUISINE
24 Broad Street
Nantucket
228-2552
Lunch Noon–2PM
Dinner 6PM–10PM
AVERAGE DINNER FOR TWO: $85

Without a doubt, Le Languedoc is one of the locals' most popular restaurants—and with good reason. Located in the historic district, Le Languedoc is located in a refurbished home that consists of an upstairs dining room, a bistro-style café and the garden terrace.

Specializing in American and Continental cuisine, Le Languedoc takes the genre beyond the basics, presenting dishes that are fresh and simply prepared—with a great deal of imagination.

Seafood variations are featured daily. The traditional dishes are delicious; the innovative dishes are surprisingly good. Favorites are Roast Rack of Lamb with a Honey-Mustard Crust and Garlic Bread Pudding, Soft-Shell Crabs and Tenderloin of Beef in a Burgundy Wine Sauce.

CHEF NEIL GRENNAN'S MENU FOR EIGHT

Soft Shell Crab

Oyster and Brie Soup

Salad Greens with Herbal Vinaigrette

Soft Shell Crab

Clean the soft shell crabs by making a cut just below the eyes to remove the face with scissors. Lift the shell to remove the gills and innards. Leave the legs and claws. What's left is edible.

Dredge the crabs in flour and sauté them in hot peanut oil. Remove the crabs from the pan and discard the oil.

In the same saucepan, combine the shallots, garlic, 4 Tbsps. butter, Worcestershire sauce, brandy, tomato, capers, lemon juice, mustard and white wine. Reduce by half. Add the clam juice and 4 Tbsps. butter. Cook until the mixture coats the back of a spoon.

Ladle the sauce over the soft shell crabs. Garnish with parsley.

Serves 8
Preparation Time:
40 Minutes

16 soft shell crabs
   Flour
¼ cup peanut oil
 1 shallots, chopped fine
 2 garlic cloves, chopped fine
 8 Tbsps. (1 stick) unsalted butter
 1 Tbsp. Worcestershire sauce
¼ cup brandy
 1 tomato, peeled, seeded, chopped
½ Tbsp. capers
 2 Tbsps. lemon juice
 1 tsp. mustard
¼ cup white wine
½ cup clam juice
   Parsley, garnish

❖

Oyster and Brie Soup

Serves 8
Preparation Time:
40 Minutes

3 dozen oysters in their
 liquid
6 cups cold water
16 Tbsps. (2 sticks)
 unsalted butter
½ cup all-purpose flour
1 cup celery, chopped
1 cup onion, chopped
½ tsp. white pepper
½ tsp. cayenne
1 lb. brie cheese, cut into
 small wedges, skin off
2 cups heavy cream
½ cup champagne
¼ cup dry sherry

earing work gloves or using a heavy cloth, hold the oyster with the hinge of the oyster away from your body. Insert the tip of a shucking knife in the hinge and twist it to open shell. Slide the knife along the inside of upper shell to sever the muscle that attaches it to the flesh. Discard the upper shell. Slide the knife under the flesh to sever the bottom muscle. Reserve oysters and their liquid.

In a large soup pot, melt 8 Tbsps. butter. Add the celery, onions, white pepper and cayenne. Stir and cook over low heat until vegetables begin to soften.

Over low heat, make a roux by combining 8 Tbsps. melted butter and flour to make a base for thickening the soup. Cook at least 2 minutes, stirring constantly, so the floury taste is eliminated. Add the roux and the cheese to the soup pot. Add the water, cream, oysters and their liquid. Simmer soup until the oysters begin to curl. Add the champagne and sherry and heat through.

Salad Greens with Herbal Vinaigrette

Whisk the mustard, vinegar, sugar, salt, pepper, lemon juice and wine together in a small bowl.

Slowly drizzle in the olive oil, whisking constantly, until the vinaigrette has thickened. Add tarragon, chives and dill and blend thoroughly.

Pour over lettuce greens and toss to coat.

Serves 8
Preparation Time:
  15 Minutes

  2 Tbsps. Dijon mustard
  ⅛ cup tarragon vinegar
     Pinch of sugar
     Salt and pepper to taste
  ⅛ cup lemon juice
  ¼ cup white wine
  2 cups extra virgin olive oil
  2 Tbsps. fresh tarragon
  2 Tbsps. chives
  2 Tbsps. dill
  1½ lbs. assorted lettuce greens

❖

THE SECOND STORY

INTERNATIONAL CUISINE
1 South Beach Street
Nantucket
228-3471
Dinner 6:30PM–9:30PM
AVERAGE DINNER FOR TWO: $70

L ocated across from the harbor, The Second Story is a charming and romantic restaurant tucked in the second story of a building. Patricia Tyler and David Toole, the
chef-proprietors of the restaurant, serve international cuisine that includes
Mexican-Spanish, French, Italian and Oriental. The dining room is decorated in Nantucket
green and pink, and is gently lit by the warm light of hurricane lamps.

The menu changes nightly and offers such entrées as Swordfish Stuffed with Smoked
Salmon Mousse and a Roast Duckling with Sweet and Sour Raspberry Sauce. Great begin-
nings are Grilled Shrimp and Cucumber Soup with Coriander or a Smoked Scallop, Spinach
and Lobster Pâté. Enticing desserts include a Chocolate Mousse Pie and a Puff Pastry filled
with Pears and topped with Caramel Sauce.

CHEF DAVID TOOLE'S MENU FOR SIX

Smoked Scallop, Spinach and Lobster Pâté

Salad of Romaine, Red Cabbage and Endive

Duck and Wild Mushroom Raviolis with Lemon Curry Sauce

Smoked Scallop, Spinach and Lobster Pâté with Red Pepper Vinaigrette

Make the pâté, in a food processor by combining the smoked scallops, fresh scallops, 1 Tbsp. shallots, thyme, nutmeg, salt, pepper, 1 egg, 1 cup cream, and 1 Tbsp. flour. Process the ingredients, remove to a mixing bowl and set aside.

In the processor, blend the lobster meat, the white fish, 2 Tbsps. shallots, tarragon, allspice, salt and pepper to taste, 1 egg, cayenne, 1 cup cream, and 1 Tbsp. flour. Process ingredients and set aside.

Purée cooked spinach with 1 egg, 1 tsp. garlic, salt and pepper.

Layer the three pâtés in a loaf pan cover and bake in a bain-marie for 1 hour or until firm.

Prepare the vinaigrette by blending 2 eggs in a processor until creamy. Slowly add the oil, red peppers, 1 tsp. garlic, fish stock and white vinegar. Serve the vinaigrette with pâté slices.

Serves 6
Preparation Time:
 1½ Hours
Pre-heat oven to 350°

- ¾ lb. smoked scallops
- ½ lb. fresh scallops
- 3 Tbsps. shallots
- ⅛ tsp. thyme
- ⅛ tsp. nutmeg
  Salt and pepper to taste
- 5 eggs
- 2 cups heavy cream
- 2 Tbsps. flour
- ¾ lb. lobster meat
- ½ lb. firm white fish, halibut, bass, etc.
- ⅛ tsp. tarragon
- ⅛ tsp. ground allspice
- ⅛ tsp. cayenne
- 1 bunch spinach, cooked
- 2 tsps. garlic, diced
- 2 cups oil
- 1½ cups red peppers, roasted, diced
- ¼ cup fish stock
- ¼ cup white vinegar

❖

Romaine, Red Cabbage and Endive Salad

Serves 6
Preparation Time:
10 Minutes

1 head romaine, coarsely
   chopped
2 cups red cabbage, sliced
1 head endive, coarsely
   chopped
1 can hearts of palm,
   12 oz., sliced
1 egg
2 Tbsps. soybean oil
1 tsp. sesame oil
1 tsp. garlic, chopped
¼ tsp. fresh ginger, grated
1 Tbsp. soy sauce
2 Tbsps. mustard
1 cup red wine vinegar

I n a salad bowl, combine the romaine, red cabbage, endive and hearts of palm.

In a separate bowl, prepare the dressing by blending 1 egg with soybean oil and sesame oil. Add the garlic, ginger, soy sauce, mustard and vinegar. Whisk thoroughly.

Pour the vinaigrette over the lettuce mixture and toss until coated lightly.

❖

Duck and Wild Mushroom Raviolis with Lemon Curry Sauce

Grind duck in a food processor. Soak the porcini mushrooms until soft and chop coarsely. Sauté the duck, mushrooms, 2 Tbsps. garlic, shallots, ¼ tsp. each cardamom and cinnamon, 1 Tbsp. ginger, cilantro and jalapeños in peanut oil. Add the soy sauce and 1 Tbsp. fish sauce and cook briefly until duck turns brown. Crack egg into mixture and mix thoroughly.

In a small bowl, combine the cornstarch and water.

Place 1 tsp. of the duck mixture in the center of each won ton and brush sides with the cornstarch mixture, place another won ton on top and seal.

In a saucepan combine the coconut cream, peanut butter, lemon juice, sugar, 1 Tbsp. fish sauce, fish stock, curry, 2 Tbsps. ginger, 1½ tsps. cinnamon, 1½ tsps. cardamom, cloves, coriander, and 1 Tbsp. garlic. Simmer until thoroughly blended.

Blanch the raviolis in the lemon curry sauce and serve.

Serves 6
Preparation Time:
** 45 Minutes**

- 2 **duck breasts, 8 oz. each**
- 2 **cups dried porcini mushrooms**
- 3 **Tbsps. garlic, chopped**
- 2 **Tbsps. shallots, chopped**
- 1¾ **tsps. ground cardamom**
- 1¾ **tsps. ground cinnamon**
- 3 **Tbsps. ginger**
- 1 **cup cilantro, chopped**
- ½ **Tbsp. jalapeños or serranos, chopped**
- 1 **tsp. peanut oil**
- ¼ **cup soy sauce**
- 2 **Tbsps. fish sauce**
- 1 **egg**
- 1 **package won ton wrappers**
- 2 **Tbsps. cornstarch**
- 2 **Tbsps. water**
- 1 **can coconut cream, 15 oz.**
- 1 **Tbsp. peanut butter**
- 1 **cup lemon juice**
- ½ **cup sugar**
- 3 **cups rich fish stock**
- 3 **Tbsps. curry powder**
- ½ **Tbsp. ground cloves**
- 1 **cup fresh coriander, chopped**

❖

THE SCONSET CAFÉ

AMERICAN BISTRO CUISINE
Post Office Square
Siasconset, Nantucket
257-4008
Breakfast, Lunch and Dinner 8:30AM–10PM
AVERAGE DINNER FOR TWO: $55

Chef/owner, Pamela McKinstry, has been serving breakfast, lunch and dinner at The Sconset Café for the past 11 years. Located in the center of the village of Siasconset, 7½ miles from downtown Nantucket, the café is adorned with chintz fabrics and local art.

The menu changes nightly and focuses on poignant dishes with local seafood and fresh produce. A feature of the café are Pamela's creative desserts, which are guaranteed to surprise and delight the diner.

Pamela began her culinary career in 1979 when she opened the Morning Glory Café on Nantucket Island. She is the author of three cookbooks which highlight the food she serves at the Sconset Café, and has recently collaborated on an African cookbook entitled "The Elephant's Kitchen."

CHEF PAMELA MCKINSTRY'S MENU FOR EIGHT

Crabcakes with Remoulade Sauce

Grilled Chicken Prego

Coeur à la Crème

Crabcakes with Remoulade Sauce

Purée the raw shrimp to paste in a food processor. Add the egg white and cream, pulse to blend. Transfer to a bowl and add the crab. Blend in the Worcestershire, salt, pepper, mayonnaise, parsley, Tabasco, cayenne and lemon juice.

Heat the olive oil in a small skillet and sauté the shallots, scallions and peppers for 3 minutes or until soft but not mushy. Add to the mousse, combine well, then refrigerate, covered, for at least two hours or overnight.

Place the breadcrumbs on a plate. Form the cold crab mixture into small cakes and press into the bread crumbs to form a thin coating. Heat the butter in a non-stick skillet. When hot, add the crab cakes and sauté over medium heat for 4 minutes. Carefully flip crab cakes and continue cooking for another 2 to 3 minutes.

Serve with a dollop of Remoulade Sauce (recipe follows) and garnish with a lemon wedge.

**Serves 4 as an entree
6 to 8 as an appetizer
Preparation Time:
 40 Minutes
(note refrigeration time)**

½ lb. raw shrimp, peeled, deveined
1 egg white
¾ cup heavy cream
1 lb. crabmeat, well drained
2 tsps. Worcestershire sauce
¼ tsp. each salt and pepper
¼ cup mayonnaise
½ cup parsley, finely chopped
½ tsp. Tabasco
¼ tsp. cayenne
1 Tbsp. lemon juice
2 Tbsps. olive oil
2 shallots, minced
1 bunch scallions, minced
⅓ cup each, yellow, red and orange pepper, minced
2 cups bread crumbs
¼ cup clarified butter
Remoulade sauce, recipe follows
Lemon wedge garnish

❖

Remoulade Sauce

Yields: 2 Cups
Preparation Time:
  15 Minutes

2 egg yolks
1 Tbsp. Dijon mustard
1 Tbsp. tarragon vinegar
¼ tsp. salt
  Freshly ground pepper
½ cup olive oil
1 cup vegetable oil
½ tsp. Tabasco
¼ tsp. cayenne pepper
2 Tbsps. tomato paste
1 tsp. lemon juice
3 drops Angostura bitters
⅛ cup capers, chopped
1 Tbsp. caper juice
4 cornichons, finely
  minced
2 Tbsps. heavy cream
1 Tbsp. minced parsley

I n a mixing bowl, whisk together the yolks, mustard, vinegar, salt and pepper. Add the olive and vegetable oils very slowly, drop by drop at first, whisking constantly. You may add the oils a bit faster after the first ½ cup has been incorporated.

To this mayonnaise base, add the remaining ingredients, blending well. Refrigerate a maximum of 4 days.

Trade Secret: This tasty piquant sauce complements cold seafood beautifully as well as the crab cake for which it was devised. If you are pressed for time, use a good quality commercial mayonnaise and add the seasonings.

Grilled Chicken Prego

Prepare the marinade in a small glass jar or non-reactive bowl by combining the garlic, lemon juice, oil, salt and pepper and tarragon. Shake or whisk to blend.

Pound each chicken breast half between sheets of plastic wrap, using a meat tenderizer or rolling pin. The object is to flatten the chicken to a uniform thickness, ¼″ to ⅜″ thick, so that the meat will cook quickly and evenly.

Place in a shallow glass or plastic container and add the marinade. Refrigerate, loosely covered with plastic wrap, for at least two hours, turning the chicken once.

Heat your barbecue to its highest setting. Set the grill about 2″ above the flame and arrange the chicken breasts so that they do not touch. Grill for 3 minutes and then turn and cook another 2 minutes on the other side. Do not overcook. Serve immediately.

Serves 8
Preparation Time:
   35 Minutes

   8 **halved chicken**
      breasts, skinned,
      boned
   6 **garlic cloves, minced**
      Juice of 6 lemons
1½ **cups olive oil**
   1 **tsp. salt**
   ½ **tsp. white pepper**
   1 **Tbsp. tarragon, dried**

Coeur à la Crème

Serves 8
Preparation Time:
40 Minutes
(note refrigeration time)

1 **cup cream cheese,**
   softened
1½ **cups heavy cream**
¾ **cup powdered sugar**
½ **cup white chocolate,**
   melted
   Cheesecloth
8 **heart-shaped molds,**
   4 oz. each
   Strawberry sauce,
   recipe follows

Beat the cream cheese with ½ cup heavy cream and the sugar until it is fluffy. Add the melted chocolate and beat until smooth. Whip the remaining 1 cup of heavy cream until stiff. Then fold the cream into the cream cheese mixture.

Line the eight molds with a double layer of dampened cheesecloth, allowing the edges of the cheesecloth to extend beyond the sides of the molds. You want enough excess cloth to totally enclose the filling.

Spoon ½ cup of the filling into each mold, smooth the surface and then fold the cheesecloth over the top to cover the filling. Refrigerate the molds on a baking tray overnight.

Serve with the strawberry sauce, recipe follows.

Strawberry Sauce

R eserve 8 perfect strawberries for garnish and purée the remainder. Strain the purée through a sieve into a bowl, add the strawberry liqueur and lemon juice. Add sugar according to taste.

Starting just below the stem of the reserved strawberries, make 4 or 5 thin cuts down the length of each strawberry, taking care not to detach any of the slices you are creating. Gently push against the strawberries to fan the cut sections.

To serve, spread a pool of berry sauce on eight individual plates. Carefully unmold the coeurs, removing the cheesecloth. Center the desserts on each plate and garnish with a fanned strawberry and mint leaf.

Trade Secret: Pair any fruit sauce with the coeurs. At the Café, we use 2 sauces on the same plate for a more dramatic presentation.

1 **pt. fresh strawberries**
2 **Tbsps. strawberry liqueur**
1 **tsp. lemon juice**
  Sugar to taste
8 **mint leaves**

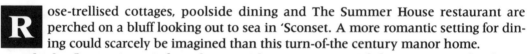

THE SUMMER HOUSE

NEW ENGLAND CUISINE
South Bluff
Siasconset, Nantucket
257-9976
Lunch at poolside Noon–3PM
Dinner 6:30PM–10PM
AVERAGE DINNER FOR TWO: $80

Rose-trellised cottages, poolside dining and The Summer House restaurant are perched on a bluff looking out to sea in 'Sconset. A more romantic setting for dining could scarcely be imagined than this turn-of-the century manor home.

The bar/lounge is an informal area with piano music nightly in season. The dining room carries the 40's beach look with whitewashed walls and floors, wicker furniture, rose and light green linens, fresh flowers and hanging plants and good 'Sconset oils and watercolor scenes.

Superb cuisine is served at this prime location by Chef Jeff Worster. The Nantucket of yesterday is relived at The Summer House.

CHEF JEFF WORSTER'S MENU FOR EIGHT

Roasted Tomato Soup with Miniature Herb Profiteroles

Greens in a Citrus Champagne Vinaigrette with Chèvre Croutons

Nutmeg Pecan Crusted Swordfish with Corn & Bacon Risotto

Roasted Tomato Soup
with Miniature Herb Profiteroles

Roast the tomatoes on a sheet pan in a 350° oven for 30 minutes. Set aside.

In a soup pot, heat the oil over medium heat. Add the carrots, celery, onions, allspice, red pepper flakes, peppercorns, coriander seeds, cloves, fennel and ginger. Brown lightly, stirring frequently. When the vegetables begin to caramelize, pour in the sherry and reduce by half. Add the red wine and reduce by half. Gently stir in the tomato paste, crushed tomatoes and roasted tomatoes. Bring to a boil and simmer for one hour.

Remove from heat, purée and pass through a medium sieve. The soup will be quite thick. Return to heat and add chicken stock to thin to desired consistency.

To make the profiteroles, bring the water, butter and salt to a boil over high heat. Transfer to a food processor or while using a hand electric mixer, add the flour and process until flour is completely incorporated. Add the eggs, one at a time. The dough mixture will be quite thick. Add the basil and transfer to a pastry bag with a small plain tip. Pipe the dough into one-inch dollops onto a lightly oiled baking sheet. Bake in a 350° oven until browned, about 15 minutes.

To serve, garnish each bowl of soup with five or six profiteroles.

Serves 8
Preparation Time:
  1½ Hours
Pre-heat oven to 350°

  8 **large, ripe tomatoes**
 ½ **cup extra virgin olive oil**
  2 **carrots, chopped**
  2 **celery stalks, chopped**
  2 **onions, chopped**
  1 **tsp. allspice**
  1 **tsp. crushed red pepper flakes**
  6 **each, whole peppercorns, coriander seed, cloves, fennel**
 ¼ **cup ginger, chopped**
 ½ **cup sherry**
  2 **cups red wine**
 ½ **cup tomato paste**
  2 **cups canned crushed tomatoes**
  1 **qt. fresh chicken stock (or substitute V-8 juice)**
  1 **cup water**
  6 **Tbsps. (¾ stick) butter**
 ½ **cup flour, sifted**
  4 **whole eggs**
  1 **Tbsp. basil, chopped**
    Pinch of salt

Greens in Citrus and Champagne Vinaigrette with Chèvre Croutons

Serves 8
Preparation Time:
  1½ Hours
Pre-heat oven to 325°

  1 lb. mixed salad greens
    Zest and juice of 2 each:
    lemons, limes, oranges
  ½ cup champagne vinegar
  1 Tbsp. shallots, chopped
  1 tsp. freshly ground
    pepper
  ½ tsp. sugar
  ¼ cup champagne
  1 tsp. kosher salt
  ½ loaf French bread
    Butter
  ¼ cup extra virgin olive oil
  6 oz. Chèvre, sliced into
    ½" slices

I n a large salad bowl, combine zest and juice of the lemons, limes and oranges with the champagne vinegar, shallots, pepper, sugar and champagne. Season with salt to taste. Allow dressing to marinate for one hour.

Prepare the croutons by slicing the French bread into ½" thick rounds. Butter each round and bake in a 325° oven until browned. Set aside to cool.

Before serving, whisk oil into dressing, add greens and toss well. Reheat croutons with Chèvre in oven for five minutes. Divide greens onto individual plates and top with warm croutons.

❖

Pecan & Nutmeg Crusted Swordfish with a Corn & Bacon Risotto

Brush swordfish filets on one side with olive oil. Set aside.

Roast the pecans on a sheet pan for 10 minutes in a hot oven. Cool and purée in a food processor with nutmeg until finely chopped.

On a flat working surface, press the oiled side of the filet onto the pecans.

Set aside and refrigerate.

To prepare the risotto, heat butter in a heavy 4 qt. saucepan over low heat. Add onions and sauté until translucent. Add the rice and stir with a wooden spoon until coated with butter (be careful not to brown rice).

Add wine ½ cup at a time, stirring frequently after each addition, allowing the rice to almost completely absorb the wine before adding more. After approximately 45 minutes when all of the wine has been absorbed, add corn, bacon, cheese, heavy cream, basil and salt to taste.

Sauté each filet in a cast iron skillet with a little olive oil, pecan side down over low heat, until the pecans are lightly browned. Turn and continue cooking until just cooked through.

Serve the corn and bacon risotto under each swordfish filet.

Serves 8
Preparation Time:
  45 Minutes
Pre-heat oven to 450°

- 8 swordfish filets
- ½ cup extra virgin olive oil
- 1 cup jumbo pecan halves
- ½ tsp. nutmeg
  Salt and pepper to taste
- 2 Tbsps. unsalted butter
- 1 onion, chopped
- 1½ cups arborio rice
- 4 cups white wine
- 2 cups cooked corn kernels
- 1 cup cooked bacon, crumbled
- ½ cup Parmesan cheese, grated
- ¾ cups heavy cream
- 2 Tbsps. fresh basil, chopped

❖

TOPPER'S AT THE WAUWINET

NEW AMERICAN CUISINE
120 Wauwinet Road
Nantucket
228-8768
Breakfast 8AM–10:30PM
Lunch Noon–2PM
Dinner 6PM–9PM
AVERAGE DINNER FOR TWO: $80

T opper's is an entirely new component of The Wauwinet Inn. Over a two-year period, the 19th-century inn was virtually rebuilt from the foundation up. The decor as well as fine food attract a stylish clientele to this bastion of easygoing class.

Menu items are innovative combinations of the freshest seafoods, meats, poultry, fruits and vegetables without heavy butter and cream sauces. Among Chef Peter Wallace's seafood dishes are Lobster and Crab Cakes with roasted Corn, Jalapeño Olives and Mustard Sauce, Sautéed Lobster with Citrus, Wild Mushrooms and Roasted Peppers, Grilled Swordfish with Saffron, Orange and Sesame Seed Butter and Wild Turkey Hash. Joining Lobster and Crab Cakes as consistent favorites on Topper's menus are the chowder, Grilled Baby Pizzas, Roast Rack of Lamb, Cool Gazpacho Verde and Fried Calamari with Torn Island Greens.

Topper's wine list consists of more than 500 selections of California, French and Oregon wines. While many of the choices are old favorites, a significant proportion are quality wines from boutique vineyards. An eight-bottle Cruvinet permits three or six-ounce samples of vertical vintage wines. The selection of half bottles on the list is the largest on the island. Vintner dinners, evenings of sampling wines with a noted winemaker, are offered three times a year.

CHEF PETER WALLACE'S MENU FOR FOUR

Lobster Crabcakes with Mustard Sauce

Caesar Salad

Turkey Hash

Lobster Crabcakes with Mustard Sauce

Mix together the seafood with peppers, scallions, onions and bread crumbs. Set aside.

In a mixing bowl, beat the egg yolk with the mustard and vinegar.

Slowly add the peanut oil to emulsify. Stir in the capers, salt and pepper. Add the seafood mixture and combine. Shape into 12 to 14 cakes.

Melt butter in a medium skillet, and cook the cakes over medium-high heat until golden brown, about 2 minutes on each side. Drain on paper towels and serve.

Serves 4
Preparation Time:
 30 Minutes

1 cup crab meat
1 cup lobster meat, diced
¼ cup red peppers, diced
¼ cup yellow peppers, diced
1 bunch scallions, sliced thin
¼ cup sweet red onions, diced
1 cup bread crumbs
1 egg yolk
1 Tbsp. Dijon mustard
1 Tbsp. sherry vinegar
1 Tbsp. peanut oil
1 Tbsp. capers
 Salt and pepper to taste
4 Tbsps. butter (½ stick)

❖

Caesar Salad

Serves 4
Preparation Time:
 15 Minutes

1 tsp. red wine vinegar
1 tsp. Worcestershire
 sauce
3 Tbsps. lemon juice
1 Tbsp. Dijon mustard
2 garlic cloves, minced
1 egg yolk
1 whole egg
¼ cup anchovies, rinsed,
 chopped
⅔ cup virgin olive oil
 Tabasco sauce to taste
1 tsp. cracked black
 pepper
1 large head romaine
 lettuce
¼ cup asiago cheese,
 shredded
¼ cup romano cheese,
 shredded

C ombine the vinegar, Worcestershire, lemon juice, mustard and garlic in a medium-size bowl.
Beat together the eggs, then add the anchovies and oil. Slowly add the oil mixture, whisking constantly, to the vinegar mixture until smooth. Season with Tabasco and pepper.
Tear the lettuce into pieces. Toss with the dressing and cheeses.

❖

Turkey Hash

Sauté the onions in oil over low heat until soft and transparent. Add the garlic, peppers, scallions and mushrooms. Cook over low heat for about 5 minutes.

Add the cooked turkey meat, potatoes and pine nuts. Add enough cream to cover all ingredients. Heat to a boil and simmer until thick.

Trade Secret: Serve hash topped with poached eggs on English muffins and hollandaise sauce.

Serves 4
Preparation Time:
  30 Minutes

  1 **onion, chopped**
  1 **Tbsp. vegetable oil**
  1 **Tbsp. garlic, chopped**
  ½ **cup red peppers, chopped**
  ½ **cup yellow peppers, chopped**
  1 **bunch scallions**
  ½ **cup mushrooms, chopped**
  4 **cups cubed cooked turkey**
  4 **cups red potatoes, cooked, cubed**
  ¼ **cup pine nuts, toasted**
    Cream
    Salt and pepper to taste

❖

THE WOODBOX

CALIFORNIA-FRENCH CONTINENTAL CUISINE
29 Fair Street
Nantucket
228-0587
Breakfast daily 8:30AM–11AM
Dinner nightly 6:45PM seating and 9PM seating
AVERAGE DINNER FOR TWO: $70

The three intimate dining rooms on the first floor of this sea captain's house reflect their charming 1709 rustic origins. The decor is characterized by wide plank floors, exposed wooden beams, huge fireplaces, and Colonial-style furniture. Tables are appointed with delicate English china, fresh flowers and candles.

Chef Keller describes his style of cooking as influenced by the French and tempered by California and Southwestern cuisines. Dinner begins with a basketful of rich piping hot popovers, for which The Woodbox is noted. A classic appetizer that follows may be Crabtina, a delicate mixture of king crab meat tossed with a bleu cheese and horseradish dressing or a Goat Cheese and Pesto Tart. Entrees such as Rack of Lamb Provencale, delicately flavored with herbed garlic bread crumbs and Cremini mushroom caps finished in a Beaujolais sauce, or a crisp Roast Duck served in a lightly sweet glaze made from three-berry casis. Among the dessert selections there is one specialty of the house you will find nowhere else on Nantucket: Bananas Foster. It's a delightful combination of honey and banana liqueur drizzled over fresh bananas and vanilla ice cream.

The Woodbox is a restaurant run by people who really love to cook for people who love to eat.

CHEF JOSEPH G. KELLER'S MENU FOR FOUR

Smoked Salmon Quesadilla

Medallions of Venison

Chocolate Bourbon Pecan Cake

Smoked Salmon Quesadilla

Prepare the horseradish cream in a large mixing bowl by blending together the goat cheese, horseradish, sour cream and 1 tsp. dill. Salt and pepper to taste. Set aside.

Heat the flour tortillas for 1 minute on each side to brown lightly. Spread the horseradish cream evenly over each tortilla. Arrange the smoked salmon over cream and sprinkle with the remaining dill.

Slice and serve immediately.

Serves 4
Preparation Time:
   10 Minutes

2 oz. mild goat cheese
1 Tbsp. fresh horseradish, grated
1 Tbsp. sour cream
3 tsps. dill, chopped
   Salt and pepper to taste
2 flour tortillas
4 thin slices smoked salmon

❖

Medallions of Venison

Serves 4
Preparation Time:
  45 Minutes

  8 **medallions of deer**
    tenderloin, 3 oz. each
    Salt and pepper to taste
    Flour for dredging
¼ **cup + 1 Tbsp. olive oil**
  ½ **lb. morels or other wild**
    mushrooms
  6 **thyme sprigs or 1 tsp.**
    dry thyme
  1 **Tbsp. lingonberries,**
    drained
1½ **cups heavy cream**
  ½ **cup port wine**
  1 **cup beef stock**
  1 **carrot, peeled, sliced**
    into thin strips
 20 **snow peas**
  ¼ **cup dry white wine**
    Thyme sprigs as
    garnish

T rim the tenderloins of any fat and silver skin. Cut into ¾" slices. Press the medallions flat with your hand or the bottom of a flat pan. Season with salt and pepper and dredge with flour, shaking off any excess.

In a sauté pan over medium-high heat, add ¼ cup of the olive oil and the medallions. Sauté for 3 to 4 minutes per side or until medium rare.

After the medallions have cooked, add the wild mushrooms and sauté quickly. Remove the meat from the pan, add thyme, pepper, lingonberries, cream, port and beef stock to the pan. Reduce over high heat until sauce is reduced by half.

While the sauce is reducing, heat 1 Tbsp. olive oil in a small sauté pan until hot. Add the carrots and snow peas. Sauté, stirring frequently for 3 minutes. Add the wine and reduce until it has almost evaporated. Season with salt and pepper, set aside.

To serve, place 2 medallions on each plate and drizzle the top with sauce. Arrange the vegetables on either side and garnish with sprigs of thyme.

Chocolate Bourbon Pecan Cake

O il or butter the bottom and sides of a 12" spring-form pan. Place parchment paper on bottom of pan and dust bottom and sides with sugar. Set aside.

Melt ¾ lb. (1½ cups) chocolate in a double boiler. Cut the butter into small pieces and stir into the chocolate until melted. Set aside and keep warm.

Separate eggs. Whip the egg whites until foamy. Add half the sugar and continue whipping until the egg whites are stiff. Set aside.

Whip the remaining sugar and egg yolks until ribbony. Mix in the melted chocolate and bourbon. Alternately fold in the ground pecans and egg whites. Pour the batter into the prepared springform pan. Bake for 1½ to 1¾ hours. Remove from the oven and cool.

Prepare the glaze by melting ¾ lb. (1½ cups) chocolate in a double boiler, stir in vegetable oil. Remove from heat to cool.

Remove the cake from the springform pan and place inverted on icing rack. Ladle glaze over cake and spread to cover top and sides. Garnish by placing pecan halves around the top rim. Refrigerate cake for 30 minutes to allow glaze to harden before serving.

Preparation Time:
2 Hours
(note refrigeration time)
Pre-heat oven to 300°

1½ **lbs. semi-sweet chocolate, chopped**
2 **sticks unsalted butter**
8 **eggs**
1½ **cups sugar**
½ **cup bourbon**
1 **lb. pecans, finely ground**
⅓ **cup vegetable oil**
18 **large pecan halves**

❖

*Ornate architecture
attracted many visitors
to the Mattakeeset Lodge,
Katama, Edgartown, circa 1890.*

The Best Inns

Cape Cod

Martha's Vineyard

Nantucket

Harbor View Hotel parlor, Edgartown, circa 1899.

THE BRAMBLE INN

2019 Main Street
Brewster, MA 02631
(508) 896-7644
ROOM RATES: $75–$125
AMENITIES: 13 rooms. Tennis courts adjacent. Full-service restaurant.
DIRECTIONS: Route 6 to Exit 10. Take Route 124 North to Route 6A. Turn right on Route 6A to the inn on the left.

T he Bramble Inn is a cozy spot for the traveler looking for a country setting and lots to do. Located on Main Street in Brewster, the inn is within walking distance of Cape Cod Bay. Watersports and a relaxing stroll along the "flats" at low tide are just some of the attractions of this centrally located inn. The grounds of the inn include lovely flower gardens and decks and patios for afternoons of relaxation.

The Bramble Inn consists of three antique homes decorated with floral wallpapers, wicker, brass, oak and iron furnishings. The main inn, built in 1861, has four guest rooms and a restaurant. Five small dining rooms comprise the restaurant and add to the intimate experience of the inn with only 6 to 12 people seated in each room.

Salmon with Saffron Basil Beurre Blanc

T o prepare the fish, remove center bones with a sharp knife and cut steaks in half down the center. Skin the steaks and pull out any small bones with tweezers. Slice the salmon into strips ¼" thick by 1" wide. Fold a 10" piece of parchment paper in half and butter the inside. Shape salmon strips into a rose shape on the paper and seal.

Bake for six or eight minutes on a cookie sheet.

In a sauce pan, simmer the wine, cream, vinegar and shallots over medium-low heat until the sauce is reduced by half. Add the butter, one tablespoon at a time, whisking constantly. Grind the saffron thread in a mortar and add to the sauce. Add 6 basil leaves.

To serve, ladle sauce onto heated plates. Remove the salmon roses from the parchment paper and carefully place over the sauce. Garnish with basil leaves.

Serves 4
Preparation Time:
  30 Minutes
Pre-heat oven to 500°

  4 **salmon steaks, 1" thick**
  1 **cup white wine**
  ¼ **cup heavy cream**
  1 **Tbsp. white wine**
     vinegar
  1 **shallot, finely minced**
  6 **Tbsps. unsalted butter**
  1 **saffron thread**
  8 **fresh basil leaves,**
     sliced thin
     Parchment paper

CHATHAM BARS INN

Shore Road
Chatham, MA 02633
(508) 945-0096
(800) 527-4884
ROOM RATES: $160–$670
AMENITIES: 26 Cape-style houses. Oceanfront location. Many rooms with working fireplaces and porches overlooking the gardens. Elegant restaurant on the premises.
DIRECTIONS: To Chatham, take Route 6 East to Exit 11 (Route 137). Follow Route 137 for 3 miles to the intersection of Route 28. Turn left onto Route 28 South and proceed 3 miles through the traffic circle to the end of Main Street. Take a left onto Shore Road and the inn will be a half mile down the road on the left.

Superbly located on oceanfront property overlooking Pleasant Bay and the Atlantic Ocean, Chatham Bars Inn is quintessential Cape Cod in all its facilities and amenities. Originally built as a hunting lodge by a wealthy Boston family, Chatham Bars Inn offers plenty of space and plenty to do.

Guests have the option of a romantic beachfront abode in the turn-of-the-century main inn or a garden setting in the 26 Cape-style houses that dot the hillside. Decorated in charming country motifs, most of the rooms have working fireplaces and porches overlooking the ocean or vast gardens.

The main dining room, with its touch of formality, and the beach house grill, with its unparalleled ocean view, serve some of the most acclaimed signature New England cuisine.

Chatham Bars Inn offers a secluded private beach, four tennis courts, adjacent nine-hole golf course, heated swimming pool and fitness room.

Seafood Minestrone

lean monkfish and cut into small pieces. Peel and devein the shrimp. Slice the squid into rings and slice the scallops in half.

Heat ¼ cup olive oil in a sauce pan and add the pearl onions. Sauté until onions are light brown. Add the leek and garlic, mixing well. Add the shrimp and squid. Sauté for a few minutes. Add the remaining vegetables, tomato, and fish stock. Add the monkfish and scallops and bring the soup to a boil.

Add the pasta and cook over low heat for 5 minutes. Add the remaining ¼ cup olive oil, butter and pesto, cover again and boil 1 minute to emulsify the soup.

Equally portion the vegetables, pasta and seafood in heated soup plates. Ladle juice over the top and serve.

Serves 4
Preparation Time:
One Hour

- ½ lb. monkfish
- 8 shrimp, cooked
- ½ lb. squid
- ½ lb. sea scallops
- ½ cup olive oil
- ½ cup pearl onions
- 1 leek, diced
- 1 tsp. garlic, chopped
- ½ cup green beans, cut into ¼" dice
- 1 yellow squash, diced
- 1 zucchini, diced
- 1 small eggplant, diced
- 1 red pepper, diced
- 1 carrot, diced
- 1 tomato, seeded, chopped
- 1 cup fish stock
- 10 pasta bows
- 4 Tbsps. butter
- 1 Tbsp. basil pesto

THE INN ON SEA STREET

358 Sea Street
Hyannis, MA 02601
(508) 775-8030
ROOM RATES: $70–$95
AMENITIES: 11 rooms. Complimentary breakfast. Short walk to the beach. Will meet guests at Hyannis airport or train station.
DIRECTIONS: Route 6 to Route 132 exit. Turn right and proceed 4 miles to the Airport Rotary. Take Barnstable Rd. for 2 miles to Main Street. Turn right on Main Street, then left on Sea Street.

T he Inn on Sea Street is a small, elegant Victorian inn—a bit of nostalgia located in well-known Hyannis. This 1849 sea captain's home has been restored and tastefully furnished with canopy beds and pieces assuring comfort while retaining the uniqueness of the era.

Guests enjoy a gourmet breakfast of fresh fruit and homemade baked treats served on china, with sterling silver, linen and fresh flowers.

Oatmeal Muffins

I n a large mixing bowl, combine the egg, butter-milk, butter and brown sugar, mixing well. Slowly add the oatmeal, flour, baking powder and soda. Do not over-mix.

Divide the batter among 12 greased muffin tins. Bake for 20–25 minutes, or until a toothpick inserted in the center of a muffin comes out clean.

Yields: One dozen muffins
Preparation Time:
   30 Minutes
Pre-heat oven to 400°

1 egg, beaten
1 cup buttermilk
⅓ cup butter, melted
½ cup brown sugar
½ cup raisins, optional
1 cup oatmeal
1 cup flour
1 tsp. baking powder
½ tsp. baking soda

❖

Breakfast Quiche

Serves 4
Preparation Time:
 One hour
Pre-heat oven to 425°

 1 **deep dish pie shell,**
    uncooked, well chilled
12 **bacon slices**
 4 **eggs**
 2 **cups heavy cream**
¼ **tsp. nutmeg**
¼ **tsp. sugar,**
    Salt and cayenne pepper
    to taste
½ **cup mozzarella cheese,**
    grated
½ **cup sharp cheddar**
    cheese, grated

Fry bacon over medium heat until crispy. Remove from heat to cool. Crumble into small pieces.

In a large mixing bowl, whisk together the eggs and cream. Add the nutmeg, sugar, salt, pepper.

Place the bacon pieces in the pie shell and top with the grated cheeses. Pour the cream mixture over the cheese.

Bake for 15 minutes at 425°, reduce heat to 300° and continue to bake for 40 minutes or until knife inserted in the center of the quiche comes out clean.

Crab Scramble

n a large mixing bowl, beat together the eggs and milk. Add the butter, cream cheese, crab, salt, pepper and dill

Pour into a lightly oiled 12 × 7 baking pan. Bake for 30 minutes.

Serves 4
Preparation Time:
  45 Minutes
Pre-heat oven to 350°

 9 **eggs**
½ **cup milk**
½ **cup butter, melted**
12 **oz. cream cheese, cubed**
 1 **cup crab meat**
  Salt and pepper to taste
 1 **Tbsp. fresh dill,**
  chopped

❖

LIBERTY HILL INN

77 Main Street, Route 6A
Yarmouth Port, MA 02675
(508) 362-3976
(800) 821-3977
ROOM RATES: $75–$125 for two
AMENITIES: 5 air-conditioned rooms with private baths. Cable TV. Guest fridge with mixers. Full breakfast, afternoon tea with freshly baked cookies and dinner on request.
DIRECTIONS: Take Route 6 to Exit 7. Right at end of ramp. Follow Willow Street 1 mile to the entrance marked by "Liberty Hill Parking" sign.

This 1825 Greek Revival mansion, which is listed on the National Register of Historic Places, is an elegant country inn. Overlooking a terraced flower-edged lawn, the home is handsomely furnished with elegant antique furnishings, upholstered chairs and thick carpets.

Innkeepers Jack and Beth Flanagan are gourmet cooks offering full breakfast treats such as fresh-baked Irish oatmeal bread, apple strudel and French toast with a black raspberry sauce made from berries grown on the property.

Puffy Omelet with Shallots & Peppers

I n a medium-size sauté pan, cook the shallots in 1 Tbsp. butter over medium-low heat for 2 minutes, stirring occasionally. Add green and red pepper strips and cook 3 minutes more. Cover and keep warm while preparing omelet.

With an electric mixer, beat the egg whites with water until whites are stiff but not dry.

In a separate bowl, beat the egg yolks and ground pepper on high speed about 5 minutes, until yolks are thick and lemon-colored. Fold yolks into egg whites until just blended. Do not over-blend.

Melt 1 Tbsp. butter in 10″ skillet or omelet pan. Pour egg mixture into skillet, smoothing top with spatula. Cook over medium heat, uncovered, about 5 minutes or until bottom is golden brown. Place pan in pre-heated oven and bake for 8 minutes or until knife inserted in center comes out clean.

Sprinkle the top of the omelet with the green and red pepper mixture and fold in half. Sprinkle the top with cheese and place in the oven until the cheese has melted.

Serve immediately.

Serves 2
Preparation Time:
  25 Minutes
Pre-heat oven to 350°

3 shallots, peeled, chopped
2 Tbsps. butter
½ large green pepper, thinly sliced
½ large red pepper, thinly sliced
4 eggs, separated
1 Tbsp. water
⅛ tsp. ground pepper
½ cup Monterey jack cheese, shredded

❖

MOSTLY HALL

27 Main Street
Falmouth, MA 02540
(508) 548-3786
(800) 682-0565
ROOM RATES: $80–$105
AMENITIES: Six guest rooms with private baths. Bicycles. Central air conditioning. Widow's walk sitting room. 15-minute walk to the beach. Full gourmet breakfast and afternoon refreshments.
DIRECTIONS: Take Route 28 south into Falmouth Center. The inn is directly across the village green.

I n 1849, Captain Albert Nye built Mostly Hall as a wedding gift for his Southern bride to equal the charm of her New Orleans home. This plantation-style home, the only house of its kind on Cape Cod, received its unusual name more than 100 years ago when a visiting child walked in and marveled, "Why Mama, it's mostly hall!"

Secluded from the road on over an acre of beautiful gardens and rolling lawn, the inn is located across from the village green in Falmouth's historic district.

Architectural features include a wrap-around porch, lofty ceilings, tall shuttered windows and dramatic central hallways. The enclosed widow's walk and garden gazebo are special places to relax.

Six spacious corner guest rooms with private baths feature queen-size four-poster canopy beds, shuttered windows with garden views, floral wallpapers, Oriental rugs, ceiling fans, and antiques.

The inn's special breakfast recipes have been compiled in a cookbook—"Mostly Hall Breakfast at 9."

Baked Fruit Pancake

Melt butter in 4 oven-proof 6″ ramekins that have been sprayed with oil coating.

In a mixing bowl, beat eggs then add the milk, flour and sugar. Whisk until batter is blended and smooth.

In a separate mixing bowl, mix together the fruit and brown sugar. Divide batter into the 4 ramekins. Spread the fruit in the center of each ramekin and top with cinnamon.

Bake for 20 minutes or until puffy and lightly browned. Sprinkle tops with powdered sugar.

Serve warm with maple syrup.

Serves 4
Preparation Time:
  30 Minutes
Pre-heat oven to 425°

2 Tbsps. butter
4 eggs
1 cup milk
1 cup flour
⅛ cup sugar, optional
1 cup fruit, blueberries, peaches or sliced apples
1 tsp. brown sugar
  Cinnamon to taste
1 Tbsp. powdered sugar
  Maple syrup, optional

❖

Cheese Blintz Muffins

Yields 12 muffins
Preparation Time:
  45 Minutes
Pre-heat oven to 350°

1 lb. ricotta cheese
3 eggs
2 Tbsps. sour cream
½ stick butter, melted
½ cup Bisquick
⅔ cup sugar
1 Tbsp. cornstarch
⅓ cup warm water
2 Tbsps. lemon juice
2 cups blueberries, fresh
  or frozen

n a large mixing bowl, mix together the ricotta, eggs, sour cream, melted butter, Bisquick and ⅓ cup sugar.

Pour batter into greased muffin tins and bake for 30 minutes or until lightly browned.

Prepare the blueberry sauce by combining the cornstarch with warm water to dissolve lumps. Add ⅓ cup sugar, lemon juice and blueberries. Cook over medium heat, stirring until mixture has thickened. This will yield about 2 cups of blueberry sauce.

To serve, place two muffins on each plate and spoon warm blueberry sauce over them. Top each muffin with a dollop of sour cream.

Raspberry Yogurt Bread

I n a large mixing bowl, cream the butter and sugar together. Add the egg, vanilla and yogurt.
   Slowly stir in the flour, baking soda and baking powder.

Pour half the batter into a lightly oiled 9″ tube pan. Swirl raspberry jam around the center. Pour remaining batter into pan.

Bake for 50 minutes. Sprinkle with powdered sugar when cool.

Serves 6
Preparation Time:
   1½ Hours
Pre-heat oven to 350°

8 Tbsps. (1 stick) butter, softened
1 cup brown sugar
1 egg
1 tsp. vanilla
1 cup raspberry yogurt
2 cups flour
1 tsp. baking soda
½ tsp. baking powder
2 Tbsps. raspberry jam
   Powdered sugar

THE OLD MANSE INN

1861 Main Street
Brewster, MA 02631
(508) 896-3149
ROOM RATES: $69–$90
AMENITIES: Working fireplaces. Full-service restaurant. 10-minute walk to the beach. Gourmet getaway weekends.
DIRECTIONS: Route 6 to Exit 9. Turn left onto Route 124 North to Route 6A. Turn right onto Route 6A to Brewster. The inn is on the left, about 3 miles after entering town.

The Old Manse Inn provides guests with a charming, cozy atmosphere, decorated with antiques, hand-braided and Oriental rugs, patchwork quilts and old fashioned print wallpaper.

Each guest room, individually appointed, has a private bath. Original prints and paintings hang in the comfortable gathering room, where guests can relax after bicycling, strolling the nearby beaches, or browsing the shops in Brewster.

Warm crackling fires and comfortable sofas beckon in the early spring and late fall. Cool breezes blowing through the blossoming perennial gardens and stately trees capture the summer visitor.

Dinner at the Manse has been recommended by Travel & Leisure Magazine, the Boston Herald, Providence Journal and Los Angeles Times.

Lobster Milano

Remove meat from the lobsters and chop roughly. Set claws aside for garnish.

Sauté the onions and ¼ cup mushrooms in 3 Tbsps. butter until soft. Add the rice and cook, stirring, for 2 to 3 minutes. Add ½ cup stock and stir until almost absorbed. Continue adding stock in ½ cup increments, to total 2 cups, until rice is done. Reserve ¼ cup stock. Add the lobster meat and set aside to cool.

In a large saucepan, melt 3 Tbsps. butter and sauté 1 cup mushrooms and shallots until soft. Sprinkle with herbs, salt and pepper. Add the cream and stir until well blended. Set aside.

Cook two strips of pancetta bacon al dente. Drain on paper towels.

To assemble, form two mounds of rice. Split lobster tails and wrap around the outside of rice. Wrap the pancetta around the outside of lobster meat and secure with string or toothpick. Top rice with a generous amount of the mushroom sauce. Place the lobster Milano in a baking dish moistened with ¼ cup lobster stock. Cover with foil and bake 5 minutes.

To serve, place on warm plates and ladle a spoonful of hot stock around each cake. Garnish with lobster claws. Remove strings or toothpicks before serving.

Serves 2
Preparation Time:
  45 Minutes
Pre-heat oven to 500°

  2 1½ lb. lobsters, cooked
  2 Tbsps. onion, minced
1¼ cups porcini
     mushrooms, minced
  6 Tbsps. butter
 ½ cup arborio rice
2¼ cups lobster stock
  2 shallots, minced
 ¼ tsp. Italian seasonings
     Salt & pepper to taste
  4 Tbsps. heavy cream
  2 strips pancetta

❖

OLD SEA PINES INN

2553 Main Street, Route 6A
Brewster, MA 02631
(508) 896-6114
ROOM RATES: $40–$125
AMENITIES: Full-service restaurant. 21 rooms, some with working fireplaces. 10-minute walk to the beach.
DIRECTIONS: Route 6 to Exit 10. Follow signs for Brewster. At the end of Route 124, turn right on Route 6A. Proceed one mile to the inn on the left.

As you motor up the long circular drive, the massive building glistens in the Cape Cod sunshine. Front porch rockers, old wicker, priscilla curtains and brass and iron beds evoke the feel of a summer estate of an earlier day.

Three and one-half acres of greenery and privacy surround you, yet you're within walking distance of golf, tennis, antique shops and Brewster's lovely, uncrowded bayside beaches.

A leisurely full breakfast is served in the elegant mirrored dining room or the wrap-around verandah.

Swordfish with Red Pepper Hollandaise

 Rub the swordfish with olive oil to help retain the moisture. Refrigerate the steaks while preparing the sauce.

Purée the red pepper in a blender and set aside.

In a double boiler, bring the water to a boil over high heat. Reduce the heat, so that the water is hot but not boiling. Whisk the egg yolks and lemon juice together in the top of the double boiler until smooth. Slowly mix in the red pepper purée. Gradually whisk in the melted butter in a slow, steady stream. Add the cayenne, salt and white pepper. Continue whisking until the sauce is thick.

Grill the swordfish to taste.

To serve, drape a 1″ line of sauce across the swordfish and garnish with red pepper.

Trade Secret: A commercial hollandaise sauce can also be used by adding the red pepper purée in place of the cream or milk in the cooking instructions.

Serves 4
Preparation Time:
   15 Minutes

4 swordfish steaks,
   ½ lb. each
1 Tbsp. olive oil
1 red pepper
3 egg yolks
2 Tbsps. fresh lemon juice
8 Tbsps. (1 stick) unsalted
   butter, melted
   Pinch of cayenne pepper
   Salt and white pepper
   to taste
   Red pepper, julienne for
   garnish

CHARLOTTE INN

South Summer Street
Edgartown, MA 02539
(508) 627-4751
ROOM RATES: $125–$350
AMENITIES: 24 comfortable, antique-furnished rooms. Many with working fireplaces. Full-service restaurant, l'étoile, as well as an art gallery and gift shop.
DIRECTIONS: From Vineyard Haven, take Beach Road to Main Street in Edgartown. Follow Main Street to South Summer Street and turn right on South Summer to the inn.

Nested in a cozy garden surrounded by brick paths, flowerbeds, lawns and lattice-work, the Charlotte Inn has watched over Edgartown's shady South Summer Street for over 130 years. Built in 1860, the inn was once a sea captain's home.

Plush carpets and lofty ceilings are invitations to linger a while. Warm, deep-hued wall-papers and vases of freshly cut flowers add to the intimacy. Fine English antiques, as well as original paintings and engravings grace the walls. This sort of meticulous attention to detail is one of the inn's trademarks . . . no two rooms are alike.

Complimentary breakfast is served in the open-air terrace or the bow-windowed con-servatory dining room.

Morning Glory Muffins

In a large mixing bowl, combine the flour, sugar, baking soda, cinnamon and salt.

In a separate bowl, beat the eggs and slowly whisk in the oil. Stir in the carrots, apple, raisins, coconut, pecans and vanilla. Slowly add this to the flour mixture.

Pour batter into 18 greased muffin tins. Bake for 20 to 25 minutes.

Yields: 18 muffins
Preparation Time:
  30 Minutes
Pre-heat oven to 325°

2 cups flour
1 cup sugar
2 tsps. baking soda
2 tsps. cinnamon
½ tsp. salt
3 eggs, slightly beaten
1 cup vegetable oil
2 cups grated carrots,
  about 3 carrots
1 apple, peeled, grated
½ cup raisins
½ cup shredded coconut
½ cup pecans, chopped
2 tsps. vanilla extract

❖

THE DAGGETT HOUSE

59 N. Water Street
Edgartown, MA 02539
(508) 627-4600
ROOM RATES: $65–$395
AMENITIES: Twenty-two rooms and 4 suites in three individual guest houses. Complimentary breakfast included.
DIRECTIONS: From Edgartown travel down Main Street, take third left onto North Water Street. The Daggett House is located on the corner of Daggett Street and North Water Street.

T he Daggett House offers guests country ambiance and authentic colonial surroundings. The main house dates back to 1660 when it was once Martha's Vineyard's first tavern.

Decorated with antiques and featuring a secret staircase, the inn retains an old New England feel. The breakfast room greets guests among New England artifacts and includes a large paneled fireplace and a view of a private garden

The Garden Cottage, a three-room restored schoolhouse dating back to 1820, sits on the long harborfront lawn of The Daggett House. It is a testament to the inn's claim to being the only waterfront bed and breakfast in Edgartown.

A private pier on the harbor invites guests to swim or to relax and enjoy the picturesque view.

Grapenut Bread

In a large mixing bowl, combine the Grapenut cereal, wheat germ, butter, salt and brown sugar. Add to this 1⅓ cups boiling water, stir and let cool.

While this is cooling, combine yeast and sugar into ⅔ cup warm water and let this stand until bubbly.

Add the yeast to the Grapenut mixture and stir.

Mix in the flour and turn dough out on a floured surface. Knead until dough is soft and smooth.

Return to bowl, cover and let dough rise in a warm place until doubled in size, about 1 hour.

Punch down with fist and return to floured surface. Divide into 2 loaves, knead for a few minutes and put into individual greased pans. Let rise until doubled, about 30 minutes.

Bake at 350° for 50 minutes.

Yields: 2 loaves
Preparation Time:
  2½ Hours

⅔ **cup Grapenut cereal**
⅓ **cup wheat germ**
 3 **Tbsps. butter**
¼ **tsp. salt**
⅓ **cup dark brown sugar**
 2 **cups water**
 1 **Tbsp. yeast**
 1 **tsp. sugar**
 4 **cups flour**

Pot Roast with Corn Pudding

Serves 8
Preparation Time:
  3 Hours
Pre-heat oven to 350°

   Beef brisket, about 4 lbs.
¼ cup vegetable oil
 6 cups beef stock
 2 Tbsps. thyme leaf
 1 Tbsp. garlic, minced
   Salt and pepper
 1 fennel bulb, roughly cut
 2 leeks, roughly cut
½ cup dry white wine
 6 Tbsp. butter
¼ cup flour

I n a large roasting pan over medium-low heat, brown both sides of the beef brisket in oil. Remove from heat and add the beef stock, thyme, garlic, salt and pepper.

Spread the fennel and leeks over the top and sides of brisket. Pour the wine over the vegetables. Cover with foil and bake for 2½ to 3 hours, or until tender. Remove the brisket from pan and strain the stock, discarding the vegetables. Pour the stock into a smaller saucepan over medium-low heat.

In a separate saucepan, melt the butter. Slowly mix in the flour to make a paste or roux.

Whisk the roux into the stock to thicken.

To serve, slice the brisket across the grain ½" thick and top with sauce. Serve with the corn pudding. Recipe follows.

❖

Corn Pudding

In a large mixing bowl, beat the eggs with the heavy cream. Add corn, pepper and scallions. Salt and pepper to taste.

Pour into a buttered casserole dish and bake until golden and the center is puffed, about 1 hour.

Serves 8
Preparation Time:
  1 Hour, 15 minutes
Pre-heat oven to 350°

  4 cups corn, scraped from
    cob or frozen
  4 eggs
  3 cups heavy cream
  ¾ cup red peppers, diced
  ¾ cup scallions, green end
    only
    Salt and pepper to taste

❖

LAMBERT'S COVE COUNTRY INN

Lambert's Cove Rd.
West Tisbury, Martha's Vineyard,
MA 02575
(508) 693-2298
ROOM RATES: $95–$125
AMENITIES: Fifteen rooms with private baths, tennis courts, 4-Star restaurant.
DIRECTIONS: From Vineyard Haven harbor take State Road to Lambert's Cove Road. Turn right on Lambert's Cove Road and follow signs to the inn.

 he Lambert's Cove Inn provides quiet and seclusion amid a country setting of tall pines, 150-year-old vine-covered stone walls, spacious lawns, rambling gardens and an apple orchard.

This is an inn for those who seek a place where both mind and body can be restored, far from the noise and crowds of town and city. The pace is leisurely, the mood relaxed and the style informal.

The original part of the main inn was built in 1790, as a farmhouse, and some of the hand-hewn rafters from that period may be seen in the upstairs bedrooms. In the 1920's the farmhouse was enlarged to serve as the estate residence of a former owner, an amateur horticulturist, world traveler and literary figure of note. It is in this dwelling that half of the guest rooms are located. The remainder are in a converted barn and a carriage house, renovated for guest use.

Each room has distinctive charm. Many open onto individual decks. One has its own greenhouse sitting room, a cherished horticultural legacy from the past. Many guests relax after dinner with dessert and coffee in the beautiful library just across from the dining room, which also features a fireplace.

Strawberry Mascarpone Filled Crêpes

Prepare the filling by puréeing the strawberries in a food processor or blender. Bring strawberries, 1 cup sugar and water to a boil over medium heat. Boil for 8 to 10 minutes, stirring constantly. Remove from heat and allow mixture to cool and thicken.

In a mixing bowl, combine the mascarpone and 1½ cups powdered sugar. Add ½ cup of the cooled strawberry sauce. Set aside.

In a double boiler on low heat, melt the chocolate. When melted, stir in ¾ cup cream until well incorporated. Set aside.

Beat 2 cups cream with ½ cup powdered sugar and 1 tsp. vanilla until stiff. Set aside.

In a food processor or blender, add the eggs, milk, butter, cornstarch, 1 Tbsp. sugar, salt and 1 tsp. vanilla. Blend on high for 20 seconds or until batter is mixed.

In a crêpe pan hot enough for a drop of batter to sizzle, pour in 4 Tbsps. of the batter over medium-high heat. Swirl the batter around the pan slowly and evenly. When the bottom of the crêpe is just starting to color, flip it over. Cook just a second more in the pan and slide the crêpe out onto parchment paper. Return the pan to the heat and repeat the procedure, to make 12 crêpes.

To assemble, fill each crêpe with 2 Tbsps. each of the mascarpone mixture and strawberry sauce. Roll up crêpes and place seam side down on a serving plate. Spoon chocolate sauce over each crêpe and garnish with whipped cream, chocolate shavings and sliced strawberries.

Serves 6
Preparation Time:
 45 Minutes

 1 **pt. strawberries**
 1 **cup + 1 Tbsp. sugar**
 2 **Tbsps. water**
 ½ **lb. mascarpone cheese**
 2 **cups powdered sugar**
2¾ **cups heavy cream**
12 **oz. bittersweet**
  chocolate
 2 **tsps. vanilla**
 3 **eggs**
 1 **cup milk**
 3 **Tbsps. butter, melted**
 1 **cup cornstarch**
  Pinch of salt
  Parchment paper
  Chocolate shavings,
  garnish
  Sliced strawberries

Outermost Inn

RR 1, Box 171
Lighthouse Road
Gay Head, MA 02535
(508) 645-3511
ROOM RATES: $195–$220
AMENITIES: Seven rooms, many with fireplaces. In-room telephone and color TV. Full breakfast. 5-minute walk over the dunes to the beach. Sailboat charters available in season.
DIRECTIONS: From Vineyard Haven ferry take State Road toward West Tisbury and Gay Head. In West Tisbury town center, take Middle Road to Beetlebung Corner. Go straight through the intersection to Gay Head lighthouse. Turn right on Lighthouse Road and take the first dirt road on the left.

Located at the westerly tip of the island, the Outermost Inn stands alone on acres of moorland overlooking the blue sea. Large wrap-around windows reveal stunning views of the dunes, Vineyard Sound and the Elizabeth Islands. The sunsets are remarkable here.

In 1990, Hugh and Jeanne Taylor converted their home into a first-class bed-and-breakfast. The decor is simple, with each bedroom featuring a different wood: oak, ash, beach, hickory or cherry.

Barbara Fenner is the cook at the Outermost Inn, which is now open to outside guests.

Hollandaise Sauce

igorously whisk the yolks in the saucepan for about a minute, until they are thick and pale yellow. Whisk in the lemon juice.

Set the saucepan over low heat, whisking at a moderate pace and gradually whisk in the butter in a slow, steady stream. Add the salt and pepper. Continue whisking until the sauce is thick.

Serve immediately.

Trade Secret: The trick here is to keep the egg yolks at a low, even heat as the melted butter is slowly added. If the sauce should curdle or separate, add 1 ice cube and whisk briskly until it has melted. This will bring the sauce back together.

Yields: 1 cup
Preparation Time:
  20 Minutes

3 egg yolks
2 Tbsps. freshly squeezed
  lemon juice
8 Tbsps. (1 stick) unsalted
  butter, melted
  Salt & freshly ground
  white pepper to taste

❖

CLIFF LODGE

Nine Cliff Road
Nantucket, MA 02554
(508) 228-9480
ROOM RATES: $40–$150
AMENITIES: 11 rooms, 1 apartment. Continental breakfast and afternoon tea included. Common refrigerator and coffee maker for guests. Telephones and TVs in each room.
DIRECTIONS: From the Steamboat Wharf, take Broad Street to North Water Street. Turn right on North Water Street. This becomes Cliff Road when it crosses Easton Street. The Cliff Lodge is on the right.

The Cliff Lodge is a 1771 whaling master's home located on a quiet, cobblestone lane by the docks. This B & B preserves the feeling of gracious old-house flavor with wainscoting and wide-board floors. Beautiful antique furnishings, country curtains and white eyelet linens enhance the 11 large guest rooms. Many rooms have king-size beds and fireplaces. The apartment has a private deck and entrance, large eat-in kitchen and living room with fireplace.

A continental breakfast featuring home baking is set out buffet-style each morning to be enjoyed in the breakfast room, garden terrace or on the roofwalk patio overlooking the harbor.

Corn Muffins

Mix all of the ingredients in a bowl. Stir only until mixed. The batter may still be lumpy.

Pour batter into greased muffin tins and bake for 15 to 18 minutes or until the tops of the muffins are golden and a tester inserted into the center of the muffins comes out clean.

Yields: 12 Muffins
Preparation time:
 30 Minutes
Pre-heat oven to 375°

 1 cup flour
 1 cup yellow cornmeal
 ⅔ cup sugar
 1 tsp. baking powder
 1 tsp. baking soda
 ½ tsp. salt
 ½ cup sour cream
 ½ cup milk
 ½ cup vegetable oil
 1 large egg

❖

CLIFFSIDE BEACH CLUB

Jefferson Avenue
Nantucket, MA 02554
(508) 228-0618
ROOM RATES: $145–$555
AMENITIES: Complimentary continental breakfast. Use of private beach, including umbrellas, chairs and beach towels. Daily maid service. In-room refrigerators. Cable TV with HBO. Direct dial phone. Exercise facility with personal trainer.
DIRECTIONS: From the ferry, take your first right and continue until the first intersection. Go straight through intersection and continue going straight. When you arrive at a slight fork in the road continue straight, do not go right towards the public beach called the Jettys. The road will come to a dead end. The hotel will be on your right.

Overlooking Nantucket Sound and the entrance of the harbor, Cliffside is the only hotel that offers exclusive accommodations directly on the beach, and is less than one mile from the center of town. Located on the north shore of Nantucket, Cliffside has one of the most beautiful settings on the island.

The building's exterior, with its cedar shingles, redwood trim and southern yellow pine decks, blends invitingly onto the beach.

The interior design demonstrates a commitment to warmth and quality. All the furnishings, including the beds, tables, vanities and interior doors, were designed and built by Nantucket craftsmen. A feeling of understated luxury is created with the warmth of natural wood furnishings, cathedral ceilings, subtle lighting and lovely prints by local artists.

As for superb dining, the Galley Restaurant on Cliffside Beach is an elegant French bistro, specializing in seafood, French cuisine and beautiful sunsets.

Salmon in Tomato and Dill Sauce

Peel and wash asparagus and cut each spear to the same length. Cook in boiling salted water for 5 minutes. Cool under cold water and drain. Keep warm.

Dip tomatoes in boiling water for 1 minute. Peel, cut in half and squeeze out seeds. Place the tomatoes in a food processor or blender with the lemon juice, salt and pepper and 1 Tbsp. chopped dill. Process for 1 minute. Add ¼ cup of oil in a continuous stream. Set aside.

In a sauté pan, pour in the remaining ¼ cup oil over medium-high heat. Season salmon with salt and pepper and place in the pan when oil is very hot, to brown.

Pour the tomato mixture over the salmon, cover, and reduce the heat, cooking for 5 minutes.

To serve, place salmon on individual plates and drizzle with sauce. Garnish with asparagus spears and fresh dill.

Serves 4
Preparation Time:
  20 Minutes

  1 **salmon filet, about 3 lbs.**
  2 **lbs. green asparagus**
  2 **tomatoes**
    Juice of 1 lemon
    Salt and pepper to taste
    Fresh dill
  ½ **cup virgin olive oil**

❖

JARED COFFIN HOUSE

29 Broad Street
Nantucket, MA 02554
(508) 228-2400
ROOM RATES: $50–$160
AMENITIES: 60 guest rooms with private baths located in six buildings. Restaurant, tavern, outdoor café, concierge, telephones. Walking distance to town and beaches.
DIRECTIONS: A short walk from Straight and Steamship Wharves.

T he inn's main building was the first three-story brick residence on Nantucket, built in 1845 for Jared Coffin, a wealthy ship owner. Today the Jared Coffin House is comprised of six buildings on the edge of town, within walking distance of historical exhibits and the main shopping area.

Furnished with antiques, lace curtains and Oriental carpets, the inn has an authentic Nantucket ambiance, offering comfortable accommodations.

Banana and Poppyseed Muffins

Purée the bananas in a blender or food processor and set aside. In a medium-size mixing bowl, combine the egg, sugar and oil, until well blended. Add the puréed banana and the orange zest.

In a separate bowl, mix together the dry ingredients. Add the dry ingredients to the banana mixture. Blend well but do not overmix.

Divide the batter among 12 greased muffin tins. Bake for 20–25 minutes, or until a toothpick inserted in the center of a muffin comes out clean.

Yields: 12 muffins
Preparation Time:
  30 Minutes
Pre-heat oven to 350°

  3 **ripe bananas, peeled**
  1 **egg**
  ¾ **cup sugar**
  ¼ **cup vegetable oil**
  2 **tsps. orange zest**
  2 **cups flour**
1½ **Tbsps. poppy seeds**
  2 **tsps. baking powder**
  ½ **tsp. salt**

❖

THE PERIWINKLE GUEST HOUSE

7 & 9 North Water Street
Nantucket, MA 02554
(508) 228-9267
(800) 992-2899
ROOM RATES: $95–$180
AMENITIES: Large back yard with picnic tables and chairs. Short walk to the beach.
DIRECTIONS: From Steamboat Wharf, go up Broad Street to North Water Street. Turn right to the inn.

Two adjacent nineteenth-century homes in the heart of Nantucket town comprise the Periwinkle. Several top-floor rooms command a harbor view. For families, there is a suite with a private floor comprising three rooms and one bath.

Decorated with antiques and hand-stitched quilts, The Periwinkle Guest House offers privacy in the center of town.

Each morning, a continental breakfast is served.

Hawaiian Chicken

ut the chicken breasts in half and marinate in the soy sauce, pineapple juice and garlic clove for 1 hour.

In a mixing bowl, combine the deviled ham and macadamia nuts. Remove the chicken from the marinade and cover the inside of each breast with the deviled ham mixture. Roll and skewer with toothpicks.

To cook, either grill for 20 to 30 minutes or bake at 350° for 1 hour. Baste with butter while grilling or baking.

Serves 6
Preparation Time:
  One hour
(note marinating time)

  6 **whole, boned chicken**
    breasts
  1 **cup soy sauce**
  1 **cup pineapple juice**
  1 **garlic clove, crushed**
  1 **large can deviled ham**
  1 **cup macadamia nuts,**
    chopped
    Toothpicks
  ½ **cup butter, melted**

❖

THE SUMMER HOUSE

South Bluff
Siasconset, MA 02564
(508) 257-4577
ROOM RATES: $175–$400
AMENITIES: Swimming pool. Full-service restaurant. Working fireplace in manor house. On the beach. Jacuzzis. Pick-up service from either wharf.
DIRECTIONS: From parking lot, take first left onto South Water Street to Francis Street. Turn right. At stop sign, turn left and follow road to next stop sign. Turn left onto Orange to rotary. Take Milestone Road 7 miles to Siasconset and the Summer House.

A rare treat by the ocean's edge is The Summer House. It's one of those special hideaways that worldly travelers treasure. Each rose-trellised cottage is decorated with treasures from the English countryside.

A continental breakfast greets you in the morning; romantic sunsets at day's end. The Summer House Restaurant is known not only for its picturesque location, but for its superb cuisine as well. Dinner each evening is an event . . . subdued lighting, flickering candles, fresh flowers and the piano bar, combining to create the romance of Nantucket as it truly is.

Cradled in the dunes at the base of the bluff, with access to the beach, sits The Summer House Pool. There is no more spectacular setting on the island, where one can enjoy a light lunch, sip Cape Codders and Sea Breezes and become totally immersed in the tranquility of the surroundings.

Pecan Tart with Bourbon Cream

P repare the tart dough in a food processor or with an electric mixer at least 2 hours ahead. In a medium-sized bowl, mix 4 eggs, the sugar and water together. Cut the stick of butter into cubes and add with the flour until well blended and the mixture resembles coarse crumbs. Wrap dough in a ball, cover in plastic and refrigerate before using.

Roll out the chilled dough on a floured work surface to ⅛" thick and 15" in diameter. Transfer the dough to a 13" tart pan with removable bottom. Put it into place and trim off any excess around the rim.

Prepare the filling in a large saucepan by bringing the brown sugar and corn syrup to a boil over medium-high heat. Remove from heat and stir in 2 Tbsps. butter, 4 eggs, 1 Tbsp. vanilla and the pecans. Mix well. Pour filling into pie shell and bake in a 350° oven for 35 minutes or until filling is set.

While tart is cooking, prepare the bourbon cream. In a large mixing bowl, whisk together the cream, 1 tsp. vanilla and Jack Daniels until peaks form.

Before serving, top each tart slice with the bourbon cream.

Serves 10
Preparation Time:
  One hour
(note refrigeration time)
Pre-heat oven to 350°

  8 **eggs**
  1 **cup sugar**
  2 **Tbsps. water**
  1 **stick butter + 2 Tbsps.**
    room temperature
3½ **cups flour**
  ¾ **cup brown sugar**
  ¾ **cup corn syrup**
  1 **Tbsp. + 1 tsp. vanilla**
1½ **cups whole pecans,**
    toasted
  2 **cups cream**
  ¼ **cup Jack Daniels**

❖

THE WOODBOX INN

29 Fair Street
Nantucket, MA 02554
(508) 228-0587
ROOM RATES: $110–$180
AMENITIES: Nine rooms with fireplaces in the suites. Excellent restaurant on the premises, but breakfast is an additional charge. Short walk to the beach.
DIRECTIONS: From Straight Wharf, go up Main Street to Fair Street. Turn left to the inn.

Built in 1709, The Woodbox Inn is the oldest inn in Nantucket. The proud innkeepers of this establishment retain the colonial atmosphere of the old ship captain's house, decorating it with early-American antiques. Glowing brass candlesticks in the dining rooms, low-beamed ceilings, and pine-paneled walls add to the hospitable charm of this inn.

The Woodbox has nine units in all, including six suites with working fireplaces and one to two bedrooms in each.

The Woodbox Inn is a gourmet dining experience at breakfast and dinner.

Scampi Sauce

C ombine the shallots and garlic with oil in a saucepan for 2 minutes over medium-low heat. Add the Worcestershire sauce, sherry, lemon juice, and mustard. Bring to low boil for 5 minutes, remove from heat and add the butter and tarragon. Let sit until the butter has melted.

Before using, stir sauce with a wire whisk. Lemon juice and mustard help preserve this sauce in the refrigerator indefinitely. To reheat, place in double boiler. Do not boil sauce after it has been made.

Trade Secret: You can substitute different mustards for various flavoring.

Yields: 2 Cups
Preparation Time:
15 Minutes

- 3 shallots
- 2 cloves garlic
- 1 Tbsp. olive oil
- 2 Tbsps. Worcestershire sauce
  Salt to taste
- 1 cup lemon juice
- 1 cup sherry
- 1 lb. butter
- ¾ cup Dijon mustard
- ¾ cup coarse ground mustard
- 2 Tbsps. tarragon

How You Can Measure Up...

LIQUID MEASURES

1 dash	6 drops
1 teaspoon (tsp.)	⅓ tablespoon
1 tablespoon (Tbsp.)	3 teaspoons
1 tablespoon	½ fluid ounce
1 fluid ounce	2 tablespoons
1 cup	½ pint
1 cup	16 tablespoons
1 cup	8 fluid ounces
1 pint	2 cups
1 pint	16 fluid ounces

DRY MEASURES

1 dash	less than ⅛ teaspoon
1 teaspoon	⅓ tablespoon
1 tablespoon	3 teaspoons
¼ cup	4 tablespoons
⅓ cup	5 tablespoons plus 1 teaspoon
½ cup	8 tablespoons
⅔ cup	10 tablespoons plus 2 teaspoons
¾ cup	12 tablespoons
1 cup	16 tablespoons

VEGETABLES AND FRUITS

Apple (1 medium)	1 cup chopped
Avocado (1 medium)	1 cup mashed
Broccoli (1 stalk)	2 cups florets
Cabbage (1 large)	10 cups, chopped
Carrot (1 medium)	½ cup, diced
Celery (3 stalks)	1 cup, diced
Eggplant (1 medium)	4 cups, cubed
Lemon (1 medium)	2 tablespoons juice
Onion (1 medium)	1 cup, diced
Orange (1 medium)	½ cup juice
Parsley (1 bunch)	3 cups, chopped
Spinach (fresh), 12 cups, loosely packed	1 cup cooked
Tomato (1 medium)	¾ cup, diced
Zucchini (1 medium)	2 cups, diced

Mail Order Sources

If you are unable to locate some of the specialty food products used in "Cape Cod's Cooking Secrets" you can order them from the mail order sources listed below. These items are delivered by UPS, fully insured and at reasonable shipping costs.

SPICES AND HERBS

Penzey Spice House Limited
P.O. Box 1633
Milwaukee, WI 53201
(414) 768-8799
Fresh ground spices (saffron, cinnamon and peppers), bulk spices, seeds, and seasoning mixes.

Meadowbrook Herb Gardens
Route 138
Wyoming, RI 02898
(401) 539-7603
Organically grown herb seasonings, high quality spice and teas.

Rafal Spice Company
2521 Russell Street
Detroit, MI 48207
(800) 228-4276
(313) 259-6373
Seasoning mixtures, herbs, spices, oil, coffee beans and teas.

MEATS AND POULTRY

New Braunfels Smokehouse
P.O. Box 311159
New Braunfels, TX 78131-1159
(512) 625-7316
(800) 537-6932
A family-owned business since 1945, selling quality hickory smoked meats, poultry, and fish. They also sell lean summer sausages, bacon, and beef jerky.

Omaha Steaks International
P.O. Box 3300
Omaha, NE 68103
(800) 228-9055
Corn-fed Midwestern beef, filet mignon and boneless strips of sirloin.

Gerhard's Napa Valley Sausages
901 Enterprise Way
Napa, CA 94558
(707) 252-4116
Specializing in more than 26 types of fresh and smoked sausages: chicken apple, east Indian, turkey/chicken, Syrian lamb, kielbasa, Italian, Bavarian beerwurst, Cajun, duck with roasted almonds and much more. They do not use cereal fillers, MSG or artifical flavors.

Deer Valley Farm
R.D. #1
Guilford, NY 13780
(607) 764-8556
Organically raised chicken, beef and veal. These meats are very low in fat and high in flavor.

VINEGARS AND OILS

Williams-Sonoma
Mail Order Dept.
P.O. Box 7456
San Francisco, CA 94120-7456
(800) 541-2233 credit card orders
(800) 541-1262 customer service
Vinegars, oils, foods and kitchenware.

Community Kitchens
P.O. Box 2311, Dept. J-D
Baton Rouge, LA 70821-2311
(800) 535-9901
Vinegars and oil, in addition to meats, crawfish, coffees and teas.

Festive Foods
9420 Arroyo Lane
Colorado Springs, CO 80908
(719) 495-2339
Spices and herbs, teas, oils, vinegars, chocolate and baking ingredients.

Select Orgins
Box N
Southhampton, NY 11968
(516) 288-1382
(800) 822-2092
Oils, vinegars and rice.

PASTA

Morisi's Pasta
John Morisi & Sons, Inc.
647 Fifth Avenue
Brooklyn, NY 11215
(718) 499-0146
(800) 253-6044
Over 250 varieties available from this 50-year old, family-owned gourmet pasta business.

FLOURS AND GRAINS

The Vermont Country Store
P.O. Box 3000
Manchester Center, VT 05255-3000
(802) 362-2400 credit card orders
(802) 362-4647 customer service
Orders are taken 24 hours a day.
Many different varieties: whole wheat, sweet-cracked, stone-ground rye, buckwheat, corn-meal and many more. They also sell a variety of items which are made in Vermont.

G.B. Ratto & Co. International Grocers
821 Washington Street
Oakland, CA 94607
(510) 832-6503
(800) 325-3483
Flours, rice, bulgar wheat, couscous, oils, and sun-dried tomatoes.

DRIED BEANS AND PEAS

Baer's Best
154 Green Street
Reading, MA 01867
(617) 944-8719
Bulk or 1-pound packages of over 30 different varieties of beans, common to exotic. No peas.

SAFFRON

Vanilla Saffron Imports, Inc.
949 Valencia Street
San Francisco, CA 94110
(415) 648-8990
(415) 648-2240 fax
Saffron, vanilla beans and pure vanilla extract, dried mushrooms as well as herbs.

NUTS

Gourmet Nut Center
1430 Railroad Avenue
Orland, CA 95963
(916) 865-5511
Almonds, pistachios and cashews.

COFFEE AND TEA

Brown & Jenkins Trading Co.
P.O. Box 2306
South Burlington, VT 05407-2306
(802) 862-2395
(800) 456-JAVA
Water-decaffeinated coffees featuring over 30
blends such as Brown & Jenkins Special blend,
Vermont Breakfast blend and Hawaiian Kona,
in addition to 15 different flavors of teas.

Stash Tea Co.
P.O. Box 90
Portland, OR 97207
(503) 684-7944
(800) 826-4218
Earl Grey, herbal teas like peppermint, ruby
mint, orange spice and licorice flavors.

VERMONT MAPLE SYRUP

Green Mountain Sugar House
R.F.D. #1
Ludlow, VT 05149
(802) 228-7151
(800) 643-9338
Different grades of maple syrup, maple cream
and maple candies, in addition to cheese, fudge
and creamed honey.

Butternut Mountain Farm
P.O. Box 381
Johnson, VT 05656
(802) 635-7483
(800) 828-2376
Different grades of maple syrup, also a variety
of honey and fruit syrups such as raspberry
and blueberry.

CHEESE

Crowley Cheese
Healdsville Road
Healdsville, VT 05758
(802) 259-2340
Smoked, mild, medium and sharp cheeses,
plus spiced cheeses such as garlic, sage and
hot pepper.

Tillamook County Creamery Association
P.O. Box 313
Tillamook, OR 97141
(503) 842-4481
(800) 542-7290
Over 30 types of cheeses, black wax cheese,
and a hot jalapeño cheese.

FISH, CAVIAR AND SEAFOOD

Legal Sea Foods
33 Everett Street
Boston, MA 02134
(617) 254-7000
(800) 343-5804
Live lobsters, fresh filets and seafood steaks,
clam chowder, little neck steamer clams, shrimp,
smoked Scottish salmon and Beluga caviar.

Nelson Crab
Box 520
Tokeland, WA 98590
(206) 267-2911
(800) 262-0069
Fresh seafood as well as canned specialties like
salmon, shrimp and tuna.

Recipe Index

Pasta

Fettuccine, shrimp, scallops, 50
Linguine picante, 116
Linguine, salmon, scallops carbonara, 90
Pasta, cilantro pesto, 134
Shrimp, Thai pesto noodles, 155

Poultry

Chicken breast, artichokes, shrimp, 87
Chicken prego, 191
Chicken, Hawaiian, 243
Chicken, Nantucket, 91
Chicken, stuffed, 162
Turkey hash, 201

Salads

Asparagus artichoke, 78
Blueberry vinaigrette, 178
Caesar, 200
Calamari, 169
Duckling, grilled, 69
Vinaigrette, citrus champagne, 196
Vinaigrette, herbal, 183
Vinaigrette, 41
Lobster, fava bean, 54
Romaine, cabbage, endive, 186
Scallops, radicchio, spinach, 141
Tuna, honey wasabi vinaigrette, 93

Sauces and Condiments

Tomato barbecue, 153
Tomato coulis, 66
Lobster basil cognac cream, 59
Ginger soy dipping, 102
Hollandaise, 235
Maple crème anglaise, 159
Remoulade, 132, 190
Scampi, 247
Soy ginger glaze, 156
Strawberry, 193
Tarragon mustard horseradish, 140

Seafood

Bass, mango sauce, 70
Crab, red pepper vinaigrette, 104
Lobster, 117
Lobster, baked stuffed, 38
Lobster, basil cognac cream, 59
Lobster milano, 223
Paella, 170
Salmon, buerre rouge, 157
Salmon, Chardonnay, 67
Salmon, egg sauce, 74
Salmon, puff pastry, 51
Salmon, saffron basil, 209
Salmon, tomato dill, 239
Scallops, radicchio, 141
Sole, seafood stuffed, 128
Swordfish au poivre, 86
Swordfish, cashew, 174
Swordfish, mangos, 124
Swordfish, pecan, 197
Swordfish, red pepper hollandaise, 225
Tuna Cape Codder, 79

Soups

Acorn squash bisque, 97
Asparagus, cream of, 161
Bouillabaisse, 37
Cauliflower caraway, 49
Chervil, cream of, 53
Chowder, clam, 89
Chowder, roasted garlic, 32
Cioppino, 85
Lobster bisque, 179
Melon, 58
Minestrone, seafood, 211
Oyster, brie, 182
Scallop bisque, 103
Split pea, dark rum, 133
Stew, shrimp & sausage, 123
Tomato, roasted, 195

Vegetable and Side Dishes

Custard, oyster spinach, 119
Potatoes, roast, 135
Pudding, corn, 231
Ratatouille, 136
Risotto, corn & bacon, 197
Vegetable Curry, 82

About the Author

KATHLEEN DEVANNA FISH, author of the popular "Secrets" series, is a gourmet cook who is always on the lookout for recipes with style and character.

In addition to "Cape Cod's Cooking Secrets," the California native has written "The Great California Cookbook," "California Wine Country Cooking Secrets," "San Francisco's Cooking Secrets," "Monterey's Cooking Secrets" and "Cooking and Traveling Inn Style."

Before embarking on a writing and publishing career, she owned and operated three businesses in the travel and hospitality industry.

She and her husband, Robert, live on a boat in the Monterey harbor.

ROBERT FISH, award-winning photojournalist, produces the images that bring together the concept of the "Secrets" series.

In addition to taking the cover photographs, Robert explores the food and wine of each region, helping to develop the overview upon which each book is based.

Bon Vivant Press
P.O. Box 1994
Monterey, CA 93942
800-524-6826
408-373-0592
FAX 408-373-3567

Send _____ copies of "Cape Cod's Cooking Secrets" at $14.95 each.

Send _____ copies of "The Great California Cookbook" at $13.95 each.

Send _____ copies of "California Wine Country Cooking Secrets of Napa/Sonoma" at $13.95 each.

Send _____ copies of "San Francisco's Cooking Secrets" at $13.95 each.

Send _____ copies of "Monterey's Cooking Secrets" at $13.95 each.

Add $3.00 postage and handling for the first book ordered and $1.50 for each additional book. Please add $1.08 sales tax per book, for those books shipped to California addresses.

Please charge my ☐ Visa
                 ☐ Master Card # _____

Expiration date _____ Signature _____

Enclosed is my check for _____

Name _____

Address _____

City _____ State _____ Zip _____

☐ This is a gift. Send directly to:

Name _____

Address _____

City _____ State _____ Zip _____

☐ Autographed by the author
Autographed to _____

NOTES